PRAISE FOR

THE CALIFORNIA KID

"What a wild ride! Owen's story is bold and spectacularly unique, as he navigates the reader alongside his piercing insight and surprising candor. An inspiring tale of redemption unlike any other."

—LOU FERRIGNO JR., Actor

"Take highlights from the best crime drama, the best story about someone who's gone wrong, Shawshank Redemption and Tony Robbins, and put them all together . . . and, then, you're still not close! Owen Hanson is a profoundly unique human and his stunning life path is going to inspire millions."

—RICHARD GREENE, Author and Political
Communications Strategist

"Owen was living the life people make movies about before Netflix was even around. His life wasn't for show, it was for dough."

—LUKE PETITGOUT, Former NFL Offensive Tackle,
First Round Draft Pick, New York Giants

"I thought I knew my friend, but his secret life was like something out of a movie—a wild mix of *The Wolf of Wall Street* and *Blow*. Now, he's sharing his incredible true story. I'm hoping he'll write a second book, revealing even more details of his journey after his arrest. His transformation is an inspiration, and I can't wait to see what's next."

—DEREK LOVILLE, Former NFL Running Back and
Three-Time Super Bowl Champ

"What a fascinating book...one learns the inside of USC football, fraternity life, the mob, and prison. They're all intertwined. Owen's story is remarkable... you can't stop reading it."

—MICHAEL LEVI, M.D., Team Podiatrist for the L.A. Clippers

"*Blow* meets *Friday Night Lights*: a wild, vividly-written tale of American addiction, greed, and betrayal."

**—GUS GARCIA-ROBERTS, Author of *Jimmy The King:
Murder, Vice, and the Reign of a Dirty Cop***

"A deeply compelling story about a young man's rise from a broken middle-class home to the heights of organized crime. Owen, a self-taught Kingpin with just a USC degree, had no background in the criminal underworld, but excelled in it. He surrounded himself with wealthy college kids and adapted to their lifestyle. This is the essential true crime read of the year, a tale of ambition, excess, and the blurred lines between good and evil."

—EVAN WRIGHT, Author of *Generation Kill*

"Owen's story is so intense and gripping. It's one of those tales that's so wild you'd think it was fiction, but it's all real. The journey he's been through is remarkable, and the best part is that it's clear he's on the brink of an amazing comeback."

—TRAY RUSH, YouTuber and Entrepreneur

```
LEGE FOOTBALL          124 GA TECH        -1
AY OCTOBER 3           125 BWL GREEN
SS                     126 OHIO ST*        -34.
          -6           127 KENT ST*        -24.
                       128 TEMPLE*
DAY OCTOBER 4          129 BALL ST         -5.5
IDA                    130 BUFFALO
LL   -3.5              131 ARKANSAS
                       132 AUBURN          -16
Y OCTOBER 5            133 DUKE*
     -11               134 ALABAMA*        -29
                       135 OKLA ST         -3
   -1                  136 KANSAS ST
                       137 TEXAS A&M       -1.5
                       138 KANSAS
CTOBER 6               139 S DIEGO S
E -33                  140 BYU             -27
                       141 RICE            -2
OCTOBER 7              142 TULANE
                       143 NAVY
   -20.5               144 AIR FORCE       -3
                       145 STANFORD
  -11                  146 NTRE DAME       -32
  -6.5                 147 W VIRGINI       -26
                       148 MISS ST
                       149 LSU             -2
7                      150 FLORIDA
16                     151 WASH ST         -4
                       152 OREGON ST
                       153 ARIZONA
```

FEDERAL BUREAU OF INVESTIGATION
SAN DIEGO, CA

OWEN HANSON
50825-298

FEDERAL CHARGES: DRUG TRAFFICKING, ILLEGAL
GAMBLING, R.I.C.O., MONEY LAUNDERING.

THE
CALIFORNIA
KID

ALSO BY ALEX CODY FOSTER

THE MAN WHO HACKED THE WORLD

THE CALIFORNIA KID

FROM USC GOLDEN BOY TO INTERNATIONAL DRUG KINGPIN

OWEN HANSON
AND ALEX CODY FOSTER

TURNER
PUBLISHING COMPANY

Turner Publishing Company

Nashville, Tennessee

www.turnerpublishing.com

T

Cover and book design: William Ruoto

Library of Congress Cataloging-in-Publication Data

Names: Hanson, Owen, author. | Foster, Alex Cody, author.

Title: The California kid : from USC golden boy to international drug kingpin / by Owen Hanson and Alex Cody Foster.

Description: Nashville, Tennessee : Turner Publishing Company, [2024]

Identifiers: LCCN 2024008726 (print) | LCCN 2024008727 (ebook) | ISBN 9781684420506 (hardcover) | ISBN 9781684420520 (paperback) | ISBN 9781684420537 (epub)

Subjects: LCSH: Hanson, Owen. | Drug dealers—California—Biography. | Drug traffic—United States.

Classification: LCC HV5805.H336 A3 2024 (print) | LCC HV5805.H336 (ebook) | DDC 364.1/77092 [B]—dc23/eng/20240507

LC record available at https://lccn.loc.gov/2024008726

LC ebook record available at https://lccn.loc.gov/2024008727

Printed in the United States of America

1 2 3 4 5 6 7 8 9 10

DISCLAIMER:

This book is based on true events. The scenes have been reconstructed to the best of my recollection, but some examples of dialogue, location, and characterization have been changed.

For the safety of many persons involved, names have been changed and details altered to protect their identities, livelihood, and personal safety.

To my parents, whose unwavering support and unconditional love shone brightly during my darkest days. Your steadfast presence was my guiding light through the shadows of my incarceration, and for that, I am eternally grateful.

To the loyal friends who stood by me, whose visits became my lifeline—you brought kindness and camaraderie when I needed it most. While I cannot name each of you here, please know that your support is deeply cherished and appreciated.

Thank you all for believing in me and for helping me navigate through the toughest decade of my life. Your faith and love have helped me emerge stronger.

With love,
The California Kid

AUTHOR'S NOTE

E very man's story is a love story in one way or another.

In *The Great Gatsby*, he loved Daisy Buchanan.

In *The Shawshank Redemption*, he loved freedom.

In *Goodfellas*, he loved *power*. For me, it's that kind of love story.

I never meant to be a criminal, but I guess that's what criminals say. We give all sorts of excuses as to our dark origin stories; trust me, in prison, I hear them day in and day out. We covet these excuses because to us, locked away for years, decades, lifetimes . . . these excuses represent vindication and the hope for rehabilitation—at least in the eyes of the parole board. We wax philosophical about why we did this thing or that—we beat up that woman because she was sleeping with another man, and our mother was a prostitute and our father an alcoholic. We robbed that convenience store because we lived in the projects and didn't have money to feed our kid brothers and sisters. We turned into a drug baron because we came from a broken home.

There are all these pretexts behind our crimes—I mean, can you blame us? We fucked up and landed in jail, where we spend many hours of the day alone in a cell thinking about what we have done and wondering why—because, had we not done it, we wouldn't be here. It takes humility and introspection to open yourself up to that sort of analysis. Like setting fire to a self-portrait, in the end you feel strangely satisfied, humbled, maybe even relieved.

But I'll save you the trouble right now: I'm not going to hide behind excuses for my crimes. I'm not going to pretend I was a good person in doing what I did, because I wasn't. And the one thing I will resolutely not do is feed you a bunch of lies to make me appear better than I am. When you're sentenced to two decades behind bars, you get a lot of time for self-reflection.

This book is my self-reflection.

FOREWORD

The FBI came in here the other day asking about the contents of your boxes. Obviously, I didn't tell them anything. But whatever you got in there, get that shit and get out of Dodge. That's my advice."

This was not what I wanted to hear at six in the morning on a Saturday.

I knew Frank from the local country club, which we both frequented. He was the owner of a private vault where you could store your valuables; in my case, I stored a bunch of cash and my gold and silver bullion. You could be anonymous there—just present a fake ID when you sign up. They had a biometric scanner for your eyes and your palm, like a Fort Knox for criminals wanting to hide their shit.

"You tell them anything?" I asked, pacing around like a goddamn lunatic. I had snorted cocaine out of a little gadget called a "bullet." Then I popped a couple Vicodin and downed a travel-size Purell bottle full of GHB. Anything to settle my nerves. I was scared, frantic. Freaking the fuck out. I kept picturing concrete walls and steel bars, impossibly thick and cold and inhuman. If a plant can't grow in such a room, how could a man survive in it? For weeks, I'd been suspicious the Feds were following me, but that's all it was: suspicion. Now, Frank was confirming my worst fears.

"Of course not, dude," he said. "I don't even know your real name." But he could have found out, surely. Like I said, we were in the same country club. All he'd need to do is point me out to his colleagues in the cocktail bar and say "Hey, what's that guy's name again?" "Oh, him? That's Owen Hanson, the real estate developer."

"They say if they had a warrant?" I asked, chewing my finger.

Frank shook his head. "No."

I took a deep breath. Two breaths. Three. "All right. I'll go get my stuff."

"And get out of town?"

"Not sure I can do that right now." Frank had a strange look in his eyes. I did not like that look. "What?"

He shook his head again, this time slowly. "If they've gotten this far . . . they probably know a whole lot more than you think they do. If it were me, I'd not want to wait around for the axe to fall. I'd be halfway to Mexico right now."

I went to my vault and stuffed as much as I could into a duffle bag, then climbed into my Porsche and drove to my friend Levi's house, whose brother was my accountant. "Think the feds are after me," I said, handing him the duffel bag. When he gripped it, he about fell over from the weight.

"Jesus," he said.

"I know."

"No, I mean *Jesus*, what the hell do you have in here, *barbells*?"

"Gold and silver." I glanced out his windows. *That black SUV, was it the same one I saw twenty minutes ago pulling out of the Wendy's parking lot right behind me?* "Give it to your brother and have him hold it for me. Have him put it in a safe or whatever, I don't care."

Before Levi could answer, I was out the door and back in my Porsche. I kept going over something in my head. It was a day on the golf course six months before, when I'd met a man named Al

Wilson, who I was introduced to via a business contact. My Australian contact had told me "Mate, I met this bloke who can move some serious money for us. He's the real deal, and he loves to golf. What say you boys play a round of eighteen holes and chat about it?"

A few weeks later, there I was with this Al Wilson character and his two colleagues, both in the Swiss banking business. Al was getting me liquored up, feeding me tequila shots and margaritas; and by the time we got to the eighteenth hole I drunkenly realized: *These guys are fucking terrible at golf.* That should have set alarm bells ringing in my mind; but back in the clubhouse, Al showed me an encrypted Phantom Secure phone he was using that only a select handful of criminals had access to. I had one, my boss in the cartel had one, all the cartel bosses had one. You didn't have a phone like that unless you were legit. Whatever reservations I had, that phone meant he was the real deal. He also offered me an incredible percentage.

"What numbers are you pulling in Australia?" he asked in between greedy bites of Oysters Rockefeller. The butter dribbled down his perfectly smooth chin. He didn't even notice. Didn't even wipe it away, like a child would.

"We're moving several million a month over there," I said carefully, mildly disgusted at his eating habits. Was the guy fucking starving or what? Who eats like that?

"And what's the commission your guys are charging to wash it?" A gulp of scotch. At that, he finally wiped his mouth with a napkin.

"Twenty-five percent."

"*Twenty-five* percent! Christ, man. We'd cut that number in half!"

That was all well and good, but I needed to see it in practice. So at first, he washed ten grand for me. Then he washed fifty. Then we were doing a quarter million every week. Where before it would take a minimum of several weeks just to get my couriers to process the transfers, Al was processing them in a *day*. Maybe that's why I trusted the guy, even though the plates of his Mercedes took me to an anonymous P.O. box on a background check, and even though he ate like an impoverished desk jockey who'd been afforded a seat at a nice restaurant for the first time in his life.

Al flew me out to Miami, where he showed me a huge warehouse full of cars they used to transport cash and cocaine. He showed me a hydraulic compressor that could store several million dollars at a time. Back then, I had shitty minivans I'd retrofitted for twenty grand a pop, while these guys had brand-new Chevy trucks whose fenders would pop out to reveal a hidden compartment where you could store twenty bricks on each side of the fender. It was James Bond shit, and that's just what I told my partners over in Mexico, who seemed all too eager to partner with this guy who was seemingly a money-laundering magician.

But then there was the fish market. That was two weeks ago, when my paranoia started getting out of hand. I had a funny feeling—I don't know how else to explain it. I was having cocktails with Al at the bar, and this guy at the far end kept looking at us. He was huge, all tatted up. He didn't look like he belonged in a nice upscale establishment such as that; he looked like he belonged on the back of a Harley or snorting blow off a stripper's ass.

I told Al "You know, if you're with the feds, my people in Mexico are not just going to kill me, they're going to kill you too."

Al's face lit up. I'd figured this would scare him, but it only seemed to shock him. Not the bad kind of shock, either, as I was hoping for. His expression told me *Holy shit, we got him.*

"I'm not with the feds," he said.

I pointed down the bar. "Who is that guy? He's been staring at us this whole fucking time, and he's not with me."

Al shrugged. "No idea, man. Look, you okay? Maybe you ought to lay off all that coke. It's making you, like, paranoid."

But after we left the bar, Al pulled me aside. "Look, man, sorry I couldn't say this earlier, but that guy *is* with me. He's my security for meetings."

"Why the hell would you need security at a five-star restaurant when you're just talking to me?"

"It's a precaution. That's all."

"Why didn't you mention it at the bar, then? Why are you telling me now?"

"I don't know who's listening at that bar. I don't know who those guys are, sitting around me; they could be anyone." He scoffed. "I can't mention that sort of thing in public."

But it didn't add up. I studied him a moment. "Hey, let me get a picture of your ID. I just want to run your information."

Al paused, confused. "Uh, no, I don't think so."

"Come on, just let me get your ID."

Al said nothing.

"Listen, everyone I do business with, I get a picture of their ID. It's common procedure, and I just haven't done it yet. It's really not a big deal."

But Al wouldn't give it up. Why wouldn't he? Furthermore, why the fuck did I not push him up against a wall right then, rip out his wallet, and look at his ID myself?

Lastly, there was the dinner I'd attended with him in Hollywood the week before. We'd both brought our wives along; and when the bill came, Al dutifully snatched it. Not only did he pay the $800 tab, he also tipped the same amount. *Who does that?* I thought. *Was it to impress me?* On the car ride home, my wife said that every time I'd gone to the bathroom, Al would ply her with questions about her involvement in the business. My wife, being smart, played dumb. "I don't play any part," she'd told him, "I just spend the money."

These were my thoughts as I drove to the country club at 7 a.m., where I was to meet Al to discuss our next transfer. I kept thinking: *Turn around. What the fuck are you thinking, you idiot? You have a bad feeling, so ditch the car, destroy the encrypted phone, and go all the way to fucking Mexico. The cartel will take care of you. Yes, they're the same people who threatened to murder you a year ago, but they've seen your work; they know what you can do. You have earned their respect.* All the same, it wasn't the most comfortable notion, that the only safe haven I had in the world was arguably under the roof of the world's most dangerous people.

At the country club, the entire parking lot was empty, aside from a truck with tinted windows. I didn't like the vibe, so I drove out and headed to the nearest McDonald's, where I got an egg McMuffin and waited, my eyes studying every vehicle entering the lot.

I could ditch right here, right now. Put my phone under the wheel and drive right over it. Deposit the pieces in the trash can, park the car in an abandoned lot, and catch an Uber out of town. From there, public transport to a safe house. I can get shuttled over the border to Mexico and lie low until the heat dies down. But what if I'm just being paranoid?

I didn't want to admit it, but my daily intake of drugs and booze could have paralyzed a small elephant. It was nothing short of obscene. And the more I took, the more paranoid I became; the more paranoid I became, the more I took. Glancing around, I took a vial of coke from my jacket and had a bump. Just enough to settle my nerves. That's all this was, anyway. I was out of hand; I needed to check into rehab again. *That's what I'll do*, I decided in a flash of understanding. *I'll go meet Al, initiate the transfer, then head on over to Villa Oasis and check myself in.*

Content with this new plan, I drove back to the clubhouse and was relieved to see Al's car there. The golf caddy approached as I climbed out of my Porsche. "H-hello, Mr. Hanson. How are you, uh . . . doing today?"

I frowned. "Uh . . . good. How are *you* doing today? You good?"

I opened my trunk, and the kid took out my clubs. "Fine, sir. Fine."

But I didn't like it. I stood there watching him walk away with my clubs, expecting me to follow, but I didn't. There was a rustling in the bushes, and I slowly turned my head. Two dozen uniformed agents sprang from the bushes with AR-15s drawn. "FREEZE! PUT YOUR HANDS BEHIND YOUR HEAD!"

Life suddenly went technicolor and slow motion all at once. The agents ran toward me, but they moved slowly, as if trudging through mud. Even the drone of the police helicopters overhead was muted and distant and dulled like an underwater scream.

Whooosh . . . whooosh . . . whooosh.

All light was suddenly bright and blinding, as if I'd been admitted to some perverse waiting room where the fluorescents were turned up to an ungodly opacity. I looked around as guns slowly rose into the air, their barrels pointed directly at me, the men holding them screaming words I didn't hear. I could see the muscles rippling in the arms of the agents running toward me, their cheeks jiggling, their dark sunglasses shielding their eyes from the sun that was now extraordinarily bright.

Closing my eyes, I raised my hands in the air and immediately felt them tugged behind my back and clamped in cold metal cuffs. Someone read me my rights. That's when I heard the accent—an Australian accent. It was then that I knew it was all over for me.

Al was rushed out of the clubhouse in handcuffs. He kept saying, "Don't tell 'em a fucking thing, Owen! They got nothing on us!" But I knew he had done this. His arrest was all a ruse, and he had played the perfect part. I suddenly knew why he was all too eager to tip

$800 on an $800 check—what did it matter, when Uncle Sam was footing the bill? I knew why he had plied my wife with questions, and I understood the vehicles in the Miami warehouse were just high-end drug-smuggling cars that had been confiscated by the feds. It all made sense. And in the midst of this, I realized I was going to prison for a very, very long time.

You might think I was afraid—afraid of prison, or of the cartel when they found out I'd been arrested. But that's the strangest thing: I wasn't afraid.

For the first time in so many years, I felt relieved.

CHAPTER 1

"Get your things and get out of here!" my mother screamed, her face mottled with rage.

I'm not sure what my dad's expression was. I was locked away in my room, lying on my bed in the heat of a Redondo Beach summer, aimlessly tossing a basketball at the ceiling and catching it with no conviction or care. But I know the expression on my face; it was the same dull, hypnotized look a kid gets when going to the movies, their eyes glazed over and glued to the screen, their body unmoving, like the way adults stare mesmerized at the shimmering flames of a forest fire. Maybe those flames are coming after them on the slopes of the Hollywood Hills, burning, burning . . . but they can't look away. They're hypnotized by the sudden, irreversible arrival of their fate.

"It's my goddamn house, goddammit!" my dad yelled, slurring, and probably squinting blankly at the double "goddammit" like my mom must have been, both realizing the verbal limitations Dad had when piss drunk. That's what the fight was about, of course. Like all fights in broken homes, it starts with an addiction and ends with a divorce. Or maybe it starts with a divorce and ends with an addiction. Either way, things end up remaining broken.

I have to hand it to my dad, who was the hardest worker I've ever met. He had his contractor's license but worked for a guy out of Brentwood who had a couple dozen commercial buildings. They used my dad for everything. Building, maintenance, property manager. Each morning, he'd drop me off at school, then drive an hour and a half to work and an hour and a half home when he finished. Maybe it's the monotony that got him. Maybe it's the fact that he worked his ass off six days a week for thirty-five years but could never seem to get ahead in life, like some caustic muck was always pulling him back down. Wasn't that the American Dream? You've got a wife and two kids who you never see because you're working, and the fruit of your labor is just enough to get by. But then someone gets sick or one of the kids is going off to college, and those six workdays turn into seven, that two weeks' vacation time turns into zero, and your sick days deplete. Folks become boozers and druggies for many reasons—cheating spouse, shame, depression—but chief among those reasons is the good old-fashioned American economy.

In this country, from the moment you turn eighteen, you're working in a rat race where you can never get ahead. John D. Rockefeller once famously said "I don't want a nation of thinkers, I want a nation of workers." At this game you don't ever actually *win*; you die in debt, probably alone because you turned into a miserable old bastard, and your debt is left to your children, who despise you. Maybe that's why Dad started drinking; it's the one thing they always fought about. And they were always fighting because Dad was always drinking.

"Do you even hear yourself?" my mom asked. "You can't think straight! How do you think I feel raising not two, but *three* kids? You're not even a man anymore. You're not even half a man!"

"OH, YEAH?" I heard my dad struggling to stay on his feet, his heavy work boots scuffing across the linoleum floor. I let the basketball fall into my hands one last time, then paused, straining to listen. Dad was guzzling his beer with a pronounced *Gllp, gllp, gllp.* Then he said "HOW'S THIS FOR BEING A MAN?" With his pitcher's arm, he chucked the bottle at the wall, where it shattered into little pieces. I flinched, and my mom gasped. There was an uncomfortable silence with the weight of oblivion behind it. The kind of silence you hear when someone stalls on the tracks before an advancing train, but they're struggling with the ignition, convinced the car will start.

I heard my dad's ragged breathing; the old floorboards creaking as he shifted back and forth trying to keep the hazy image of my mother within view, staring dumbly at her, daring her to be pro-voked. "You *bastard*," she finally said, but she didn't yell. She whis-pered it. In the next room, my sister sobbed quietly into her pillow. I heard the kitchen door open. "Guest room. *Now*. We need to talk."

"Oh, y-yeah?" my dad said, lumbering. He staggered into the counter, which he must have clutched to regain his footing, because dishes clanged from where his elbow pushed them.

"Yes," my mom whispered again, which is how I knew it was bad. "You're certainly in no position to talk coherently, and I don't know you'll even remember discussing this in the morning, but I sure hope you do. Because I will."

My dad seemed to sober at that, a moment. He was not a stupid man. He said nothing, as I pictured my mother silently holding the door for him, while he hunched his broad shoulders, bowed his head, and strode out into the bright California sunshine, replete with so much promise. Mom closed the door softly behind them.

Immediately, I sprang from my bed and went to the window. My parents entered the back garage where my bedroom looked on. Through the garage windows, I saw them screaming at each other. My mother's face was red, her hair falling like scimitars across her eyes. But she didn't brush it back behind her ears like she normally did. It's like she didn't even notice anything around her. Strange, watching them, both so angry, so full of vitriol, their screams muted by the distance between us. Like watching one of those old silent-era films, Charlie Chaplin bouncing around with his cane and his hat, making people trip and fall and laugh. But I wasn't laughing.

"Owen?" a soft voice called from the other side of my bedroom wall. I bent my ear to it.

"It's all done," I said.

"You sure?"

"Course I'm sure."

"Don't sound sure."

"But I am. Scout's honor."

Outside, the faint din of screams emanated from the garage as another beer bottle shattered against a wall.

"What's that?" she said.

"Ice cream truck," I said matter-of-factly. "Far away, unfortunately."

"Oh," she said, an infinite sadness in her voice.

"What, you want an ice cream cone?"

"Could really use one," she said.

"Hang on a second." I went into the kitchen and opened the freezer, taking two Drumsticks out. Then I went up and knocked on my sister's door. "Special delivery."

She opened the door, her wet, reddened eyes lighting up. "Really!"

"Shhh," I whispered, handing it to her. "Can't tell no one."

She held out her hand expectantly. "I won't! Promise."

"But there's a catch." A look of disappointment, hands on her hips. Another scream from far away, but my sister didn't hear that one. "Don't worry, it's just a small one."

"Okayyyy."

"You gotta promise to stop suckin' your thumb all the time. And you gotta let Mom wash Blankie once a week. Got it?"

She smiled. "Blankie!"

"Yep. Once a week, Mom washes it."

"Okay!" she nodded vigorously, holding out her hand. This was a small victory, but a victory nonetheless. Any little thing that could take some stress off my parents' back might keep them from fighting just a little bit; might make them hold on just a little bit longer.

I closed her door and went back to my room, then sat against the wall, eating my ice cream while through the wall she told me about her new bunny named "Buddy" in between pauses as she took huge bites. At some point there was a longer pause than usual, followed by groaning. "You still alive?" I said. I heard her hitting her forehead with her palm.

"Ugh. Brain hurts!"

"That's called a brain freeze. You're supposed to lick it, not inhale it, moron."

I listened to her talk until the outside screams faded, overcome by the traffic sounds and airplanes thundering overhead. At some point the kitchen door opened, and I heard my mom crying softly. "This is the last time," she said.

The next day, my dad didn't take me to school. His coffee pot wasn't even dripping with his classic Folger's roast. He was never absent from breakfast.

Slipping outside, I headed to the garage, glancing around to make sure my mom couldn't see me. I tiptoed inside and stopped immediately at the sound of broken glass crunching beneath my Converses. Broken bottles lay strewn all over the room, and there was residue of white powder on the coffee table. Kneeling beside the table, I smeared my finger lengthwise through the powder, bringing it up to my nose to give it a sniff. Frowning, I wriggled my nose; some of the powder had shot into my nostrils by accident. Felt like a sneeze was about to happen but wouldn't, followed by a weird case of brain freeze; but instead of pain, there was a weightless sensation. "Weird," I muttered, wiping the powder from my nose.

I ran to the house and grabbed my backpack. Mom ushered us into the car, and I sat in the front seat watching the city whirl by in a dusty haze. I felt omnipotent, for some strange reason. Like I could nail a slam dunk on the basketball court or fend off half a dozen bullies at once. Hell, I could probably even do it one-handed. Maybe even—

"Kids," my mom said, interrupting my thoughts. Turning, I stared at her, blinking. She frowned, grabbing my chin. "Why're your pupils so big?"

"I donno."

"Are you sick?"

"No, ma'am. I mean, maybe. I do feel a little weird. . . ."

"Do you need to stay home?"

I shook my head. She studied my eyes a moment, which were lolling around. Then she put her hand to my forehead. "Hmm. No fever. Go to the nurse when you get to school."

"Okay."

"I need to talk to you guys about something. Your dad . . . he's . . . sick."

"Like me right now?" I asked aimlessly, again gazing out the window. The cars seemed so freakin' *fast*. How did they move like that?

"No, not like you. But he's awfully sick and needs help, and we're not going to see him around for a little while."

"What!" my sister whined. "Why?"

"Daddy's in the hospital, honey."

My sister gasped. "Is he dying?" She was tearing up, suddenly beside herself. The sudden emotion felt bizarre to me, like I was witnessing it from far away when all I wanted was to look at the speeding cars.

"No, of course not," my mom said. "He's just ill. So he's staying with the nice doctors at the hospital for a little while until he gets better. But he will get better. Understood?"

I nodded. "Will we be able to see him?"

"Yes, in a week or so."

"How long does he have to be there?"

My mom chewed her lip. When she looked at me, I saw tears in her eyes. "I don't know," she said, wiping them away. "Until he's better."

My dad didn't look like himself.

Sitting in a hospital gown in the corner of the tiny room, he peered out from the barred window at the hospital parking lot below. He stared at it listlessly. It was an overcast day in Los Angeles, the huge, darkened clouds threatening to release rain from their bellies; but every now and then the clouds parted, revealing stray shafts of sunlight that filtered into the room. When this happened, my dad grimaced and shielded his eyes.

He was deathly pale, no sign of the deep surfer's tan my dad usually sported. And far too skinny. I don't remember ever seeing him so thin. And he kept shaking like he was freezing cold. He was never real big on affection, but he did give me a hug; the whole time of the hug, it had felt like I was cradling a small animal suffering from hypothermia, willing it to warmth and back to life. This wasn't normal: my dad was a hulking man, larger than life. Nothing could put him down. I found myself glancing at the door, wondering when my mom and sister would get back from the cafeteria.

Beside his bed was an untouched tray of food I didn't recognize. It looked like three variations of refried beans, all different colors too. "Not hungry?" I asked, breaking the silence. My dad, still staring out the window, shook his head. My belly was grumbling. We'd skipped breakfast so we could get here before the morning traffic. "Can I have some?"

"Sure, son."

Smiling greedily, I took the tray and unwrapped the plastic utensils. I drove my fork into the mush and brought it to my mouth. I stopped chewing. "What the . . . *eeew*. Why are you eating this crap?" I pushed the tray away. "Is that even *food*?"

My dad chuckled, which made me happy. I hadn't heard him laugh in a long time. "That's hospital food for ya, son. Not like what Mom cooks at home." He fell silent a moment. "You don't ever want to come here. I hope you never do."

"The hospital?" I said, wiping my mouth with my arm. "Been here already. 'Member I cut my leg skateboarding at grandma's? That friggin' sucked. Thought my leg was a goner, Pops."

"No," he said seriously. "This is a different kind of hospital. And I hope to God you never find yourself here when you grow older. That would . . . it would break me."

I watched him a moment. "But, Dad. . . ." The door opened, and my mother and sister came into the room. At their heels was a doctor. My mom smiled at Dad when she came in, but there was no joy in her eyes.

"Mr. Hanson," the doctor said. "What a wonderful little family you have here. I was just telling your wife about the incredible progress you've been making. We'll be able to release you within the next two weeks. How's that sound?"

For the first time in my life, my father seemed embarrassed. He glanced at my mom for a second, then immediately looked away.

"Yeah," he said quietly, "that sounds good."

There was an awkward pause. The doctor ruffled my hair. "And who's this big guy here?" he said, smiling. He patted my shoulder. "You look like you're tall enough to dunk a basketball."

Still looking out the window, my dad said "Owen plays just about every sport there is."

"That so?"

"Mom says I'll be bigger than Dad someday," I said proudly. But seeing how thin he was, it sucked the joy out of that statement immediately.

"I'm sure you will, son," the doctor said.

He excused himself to speak with my mom in the hallway. My sister had already jumped onto my dad's lap, talking non-stop about Buddy and her new friends at preschool. She talked as if he hadn't been home in years, when it was just a couple of months. My dad held her, smiling weakly. He seemed to be in some halfway place between happiness and embarrassment. His physical form was there in the room with us, but the essence of him was gone.

My dad had become a ghost.

In the end, it wasn't the drinking that got him. It was another woman.

They always say "I remember it like it was yesterday." When your life changes—in a moment, in a word, in a chance encounter—or, in my case, in the last scenes of a harrowing goodbye, of course you'll always remember. It's these stray moments that shape the rest of your life. That make you a man, or less of one. That set you on the path toward whatever dream or nightmare you end up following, whether it's the love or the trauma or the loss of the thing. Old-timers in dive bars reflect on these moments. You can spot them at the counter sitting forlornly with no friends in sight, always at the center of the bar so their voice can have the most reach when it says to the guy in the back trying to remain unseen, or to the couple just off-center necking, or even to the bartender: "You know . . . I had a wife once."

These are the words that bleed out of us. That bleed from our eyes without speaking, or from our mouths when we're nostalgic and in need of a free therapy session from a friend or complete stranger. It's cliché but it's fucking true. And the thing I remember like it was yesterday—the thing that made little innocent Owen Hanson a little less innocent—was my mom packing the car to head up north, for good.

I said it in the beginning of this book, and I will say it again: at the end of the day, our mistakes are our own. I've known cheaters who claim they did what they did because of their own trauma of having been cheated on. There are those who say pedophiles themselves were abused as children. There are abusers of women who grew up watching their dad beat their mom. These are shit justifications coming from sorry excuses for humanity. That's all they are—excuses. But this isn't an excuse: it's what happened, and what changed me.

I remember a strange sensation washed over me as I initially tried helping Mom load the car with her belongings. She had them in boxes and trash bags; the ones I could carry, I hefted over my shoulder and set in the trunk. But after placing a box in, I suddenly froze. Looking down at that box, I realized I was contributing to the collapse of my family. With each item of my mom's belongings, I was speeding up the process of my own abandonment. What if I stopped helping, and the packing took another couple minutes? Maybe in those few minutes she would come to her senses and not leave.

Backing up slowly, blinking too many times, I bumped into her hastily brushing past with a garbage bag full of clothes. Behind us, my dad stood stoically at the edge of the property with my sister, who was on the ground crying. "Oops, sorry, Owen," my mom said. I watched her organize the trunk—stacking records on top of a box, shifting garbage bags on top of those. *You're sorry for bumping into me, but you're not sorry for leaving me?* I decided to stop helping her after that. Too many questions in my mind were left unanswered. Big questions for a small kid. How often will I see my mom and sister? How will we survive without Mom? Who will feed us? Does she not love me enough? If she did, why would she take my sister and not me? Man, did I do something wrong?

If she wanted to leave my dad, sure. I didn't get it then, but I get it now. But move *seven hours* away from me? Can't you just move out but stay in the same city? Silly childhood notions kept plaguing me: maybe I didn't make my bed right a few too many times. Was I bad at sports? Was my schoolwork not up to par?

My sister wailing, the bright sun blinding, and my dad just watching silently, knowing he had contributed to this. Knowing there was not a single thing he could do now to save his family. His mistakes were made, and sometimes there's just no fixing what is broken.

The trunk groaned shut. My mom let out a breath and slapped her thighs in finality. "All right, all packed up!" She said it as if she was going on a fucking camping trip with friends for the weekend. "Honey, ready to go?"

My sister was so scared and sad, there was nothing she could do but sob. Clutching my dad's leg, she held on for dear life. My dad bent down, picked her up, and held her, Buddy squeezed tight between them as my sister would not let go of him, either. "It's all right, kiddo," he said softly. "Go on, go with your mom. I'll be seeing you soon. Promise."

She sobbed and choked into his shoulder. Across the street, one of our neighbors who was washing his car stopped spraying the hose to watch. Some neighborhood kids peeked out from their windows, and cars slowed when they passed us. I wanted to shrivel up inside myself and disappear into the void that would remain once they left. Wanted this horrible dream to end, and me to wake up to the smell of bacon and fried eggs and my little sister giggling in her booster seat at the kitchen counter as she played with her food, the sound of coffee sloshing around the pot as my dad filled his thermos before going in to work. My mother calling softly in singsong, "Owennnnn . . . time to wake up, honey. Breakfast!"

Where would these memories go? Would they just be forgotten? Would I be forgotten?

"Okay, honey," my mom said, growing impatient, "give your brother a hug and then let's go."

My dad set her down and she rushed to me, grabbing hold and squeezing the air out of my lungs. I stood holding her in a daze, watching the memories unfold and asking why they had to stop. But I was my father's son. I had to be strong. For her. "Love ya, kid," I said, ruffling her hair as her tears soaked my shirt. At that point, at eight years old, I'd never felt someone sobbing in my arms. It wasn't something I wanted to get used to.

The film reel speeds up then, because I want it to; suddenly they were in the car driving on down the road. I don't recall if Mom hugged me. I don't much care. I just remember my little sister waving at us through the rear window, and then they rounded a bend and were gone.

Walking up to my dad, I took a few tremulous breaths before falling into an awful sobbing fit. My dad said, sternly, "Son, we don't cry as men. Especially not this family."

What family? I wanted to ask. I sniffled a few seconds, wiping my tears as we stood there together in silence, our neighbors deciding it was best to finally leave us alone and go back to what they'd been doing, the show being over and all that. "Come on," my dad said. "Let's go to the beach."

The house felt real cold after Mom left. Dark and cold.

Very soon, I started recognizing little things I'd never thought about missing before, because I never thought there would come a day when I'd have to miss them. Things like having Mom make breakfast, dinner, and snacks when I came home from school; cookies and milk and all that good stuff. I no longer had the same comfortable sheets and comforters. The dining room table was never set; we used paper napkins instead of the nice cloth ones my mom had. The family pictures had been stripped off the walls.

At eight years old, you're used to having your towels washed every other day, and your sheets changed for you. Now I'd hold an old stinky towel thinking "This smells a little moldy." Or I'd roll around my bed covered in beach sand, feeling all the tiny granules, and wondering how to get them off my sheets. My dad would wash the bedding and towels once a month.

The biggest change wasn't all these little things, but the one big thing: my mom and sister were missing from the picture, and without them it wasn't a home but the shell of one. My mom had been loving. She used to tuck me in bed and sing lullabies to help me fall asleep. With that gone, it became hard to sleep at night. The things I heard now were my dad with a woman in his bedroom, or the TV at full throttle late at night, or one of his surfer buddies hanging out drinking. All the roses in our garden my mom used to tend so diligently slowly started wilting away, until they were all dead.

CHAPTER 2

Time quickened up again.

School passed by in a blurry haze of sports and homework, which my dad made sure I excelled at. Our home became just another place to lay my head, but not a bad one at that. My dad's best bud, Dennis Jarvis, owned a couple of surf shops in Hermosa Beach called Spyder Surfboards, a well-known brand back in the day. Dennis was one of the best board shapers in the world, and he would sponsor all these pro surfers for their California tours: Conan Hayes, Tommy Curren, Greg Browning. My dad told him "Any time you want to let the guys stay at the house, they can."

I slept on the top bunk, and my dad would rent out the bottom bunk to a pro surfer like Conan Hayes, who later co-founded the clothing company RVCA. They were gone most of the time, or else they were in the room sleeping. I'd always tiptoe up to the bunk bed, trying hard not to wake them. These guys looked like slumbering gods. I remember my dad saying "Hey, don't wake up Conan. He's sleeping today." Sometimes I'd steal glances at him, thinking how cool it would be to become a professional athlete one day. Wouldn't that set you up for life? Wouldn't it net you all the money you need, get you the good home and family, get you the trophy wife and the pool in the back yard with the white picket fence? I thought about it obsessively, sports being my ticket to all the great things, the means to crawl out of poverty to create a successful and fulfilling life. This obsession fueled my drive to excel.

While there weren't women around—well, there sure were, but they were of the transitory type—there was a sense of camaraderie, friendship, brotherhood, all through the shared bond of sports, which soon became the nexus around which my world revolved. It became everything I looked forward to upon waking each day—the ultimate means to an end—and it soon was inextricably woven into the very fabric of my identity.

I played them all. I'd head down to the beach every day with my dad and play volleyball. I'd surf alongside his pro buddies, play basketball, baseball. My dad had been a great college athlete. At his height, build, and tenacity, I always knew he could have gone pro. I think he knew it too. He used to play basketball at Pepperdine but was later kicked off the team because of his drinking. He remained a talented athlete, and, in the wake of my mother and sister's absence, sports became our father–son bond. He pushed me constantly to play everything, urging me to become the best I could be in every conceivable way because maybe my skill could land me a scholarship down the road. God knows we didn't have any money for school. I think this was my dad's way of making sure I didn't fall down the path he had. He probably also knew that if you were on a team, your teammates wouldn't tolerate you fucking off with drugs or booze. His old teammates hadn't. There's a brotherhood in sports unlike anything else—they become your surrogate family. In some way, I think my dad was making up for the family he had destroyed.

The best part was the gleam in his eye when I'd win a game, sink a three-pointer, or hit a home run. I lived for that look. He was always the focal point of my gaze at the games and practices— the way he'd clap and cheer, looking around as if proudly declaring *"That's my son; isn't he good!"* My new family was one of unparalleled excellence and determination. They were professionals of the highest order, and we didn't talk about our feelings; that's not what us men were supposed to do. We were just supposed to *win*.

In high school, my dad was nervous I'd start drinking with my buddies and smoking weed. After all, that's when it had begun for him. But I was scared shitless of the man. There's no way I'd disobey him because, for one, he'd whoop my ass. And two, that gleam of fatherly pride would fade as surely and quickly as the exhaust from my mom's station wagon as she sped away toward her bright shiny new life. I'd lost her and my sister. I was not going to lose my dad.

I also knew that alcoholism and addiction ran rampant and unchecked in my family. My grandfather on my mom's side was a heavy drinker, my dad's dad was a drinker, and he was a drinker. Everyone was boozing, and it was not lost on me that so many of their problems in life stemmed from it.

When my friends would invite me to a rager, I'd recall the time I saw how beaten and broken my dad was in that hospital bed. The shame, the sadness, the fear. No, fuck that. Drinking made sure your family fell apart. Drinking meant you'd end up in a hospital, in jail, and, worse than all those combined, it meant you would end up alone. In a rare expression of emotion, my dad even said, from time to time: "Son, remember, you're *never* going to drink." He'd say it sternly, sadly. Then casually and quickly would throw in "I don't want you to end up like me." And that was the end of the conversation. I listened to my father and obeyed him.

Then college happened.

At a certain point, a man just needs to set out on his own and learn the ropes of this crazy life by grabbing hold of them himself, without the assistance of anyone else. Sometimes, he's just got to figure things out on his own.

I'd gotten a two-thirds scholarship for volleyball at the University of Southern California, and it was as if I'd been given ten thousand bucks, a backpack, and a one-way plane ticket to Europe. The feeling was one of ultimate freedom and discovery. I'd been living in this insular little beach shack for eighteen years. I'd never really been my own man; I lived under the domineering shadow of my father, who was understandably just trying to make sure I didn't make the same mistakes he had.

It was the year 2000 when I'd gone on a volleyball-recruiting trip to USC during my senior year. After the game, the USC players took me to a party they had on campus with all the volleyball players and fraternity guys. I drank my first beer with them and was instantly shit-faced. A fat joint materialized in my hand, and I puffed on it, watching it dully like it had become another appendage on my body, a strange sensation washing over me like a staticky blanket. A dumb smile curled across my lips as I watched beautiful sorority girls walking around, a game of beer pong at full tilt, and rap music blaring from loudspeakers set up throughout the house.

The weed hit hard and fast. The room was suddenly spinning, colors and sounds merging into a mess of foreign sensations and visuals. One of the volleyball players said "Look, I think we got our homeboy here a little fucked up. You good, buddy?" He laughed, clapping my shoulder. I laughed back, but the sound was weird, tinny, far away.

"Yeah, I'm good," my voice said from some far distant location. I peered down at the joint, suddenly horrified. What the fuck was this thing? I guess my dad was right. I quickly handed it back, then proceeded to live on that couch for the rest of the night. It wasn't the best first experience with drugs and alcohol. But it certainly would not be the last.

Now attending USC, I started drinking with the fellas on the volleyball team after games. We'd head out as a team to the campus bar to have a couple cold beers. The more I drank, I discovered, the better I felt. I thought *I know what my dad was talking about now. This stuff's deadly. And I* dig *it.*

All this time, my only real release had been through sports. Through physical exertion and the natural high of a good game. Once that subsided, I just felt tired and sore. But with the booze, and then soon after with the coke . . . I felt like fucking Superman. Now as a grown man I could have the high of the game *and* the high of the afterparty, and the sensation was nothing less than euphoric. There was the whole college experience too. Me, a poor beach kid, was now hanging with the best of college volleyball players, talking to gorgeous sorority girls, and living the dream life. My dad, who had brought me up on the fraternal nature of sports, probably couldn't have imagined it would lead to this.

My sophomore year, I learned that success in any field was all about networking, and this meant cozying up to the fraternity houses and attending their parties. I came in as a volleyball player; I couldn't exactly go to parties unless they were sports-related. I noticed at all the good fraternities, those guys had the real dream life: they drove expensive sports cars, dated the most beautiful women around campus, and hosted unrivaled festivities. These guys were the crème de la crème, the future leaders and shakers of America. Some of my buddies on the volleyball team pledged for these fraternities. For a kid who'd grown up without many of the accoutrements of the American dream—a good family, a nice home, a decent car—it was a no-brainer: I wanted in on that shit.

My uncle who'd gone to USC was a Beta, which proved an instant "in" for me. Several of my buddies on the volleyball team were Betas already. Those that weren't in a fraternity were basically the odd men out. They weren't really able to go to the parties or hook up with sorority girls. And that was what college was all about. I wanted to live my college years to the fullest.

My first month of pledging, I experienced a party where I discovered what being a Beta was all about. Every sorority girl on campus wanted to be invited. Fraternity brothers were allowed to bring three dates, pledges two. This was the Arabian Nights party at the Playboy Mansion, and us pledges were humiliated by being dressed in diapers with bibs and sucking on pacifiers. Dwarves were walking around with platters of cocaine and ecstasy pills balanced on their heads.

Then, at the end of pledging, there was the infamous "Hell Week."

The Beta house was huge, a massive blocky brick Colonial with towering columns at the front, reminiscent of something you might see at the estate of an old land baron in the bayous of Louisiana. It was two stories, had fifty rooms complete with pool tables, kegs, bars, and even a basketball court in front of the building. Hell Week took place in the basement. And it was not for the faint of heart.

Hell week was a total boot-camp mindfuck. This is when the *real* hazing began. Seniors would come into the basement all fucked up on coke and order us to run in place in pitch darkness, which was how the basement was the entire time. We would be forced to do push-ups and the "human chair."

"Chair, you fucking maggot! Now!"

I'd jump into position, not allowing my back or ass to touch the walls, and we would hold our pledge brothers' hands and chair for twenty minutes at a time as fraternity members walked across us like a bridge, sometimes stepping on my balls, on purpose or accident I didn't know. If any of the drunk and coked-up members fell while walking, beer would be thrown in our faces as punishment.

"Chair, you jock piece of shit!" someone yelled at me.

"I am!"

"WELL, CHAIR FUCKING HARDER!"

He spit in my face, and I couldn't clean it off as I was chairing, so I let the saliva ooze down the side of my cheek, pooling as a gooey mass on the base of my chin and refusing to fall off. I felt it trembling there against the awkwardness of my stance, a tickly appendage.

"Jock bitch, why don't you hang out with us? You too fucking good for us?"

"Sir, I'm sorry, sir, I was at volleyball practice."

"LIES! DOUSE HIM!"

Another splash of beer. Another loogy, this one in my eye. I had to keep my eye shut because I couldn't wipe it off. Once we broke chair formation, I finally wiped off the gobs of spit. No sooner had I done that than one of the members said "Drop and give me a hundred!"

"Sir, yes sir!"

I did a hundred push-ups. Once I'd finished, someone took out a fat lipper of chewing tobacco and placed it above my top lip like I was Tom Selleck. Every member in the basement laughed uproariously. When it was time for a meal, all we would eat, or should I say *drink*, were Beta Milkshakes, consisting of buttermilk and curry, until we puked. If we fucked up in any way, or if one of the members didn't like one of us, we would be ordered to drop our drawers and the member would pound on our asses with a wooden paddle—the same ones us pledges carried around at all times. Some of the members took a sadistic sense of pride in this practice, reminding me of some of the Nazis I'd read about in the concentration camps. I felt like I was trapped in a fucking nightmare.

By the seventh day, I was emaciated, dehydrated, and delusional. I kept seeing things, shadows darting in the periphery, always too quick for me to catch them. The concrete walls and floors reeked of piss and vomit. Some of the pledge brothers cried softly in dark corners, or sobbed openly like they were children again. I hadn't slept in 150 hours. My eyes kept twitching and I felt like I had gone insane. I would never recover from this.

Once we were allowed out, I crawled up the stairs to my Big Brother Phil's room, my mentor, and he ordered me to do a Beta Vacuum in exchange for a Subway sandwich and a Diet Coke. I spent the next half hour on my hands and knees picking up trash from the floors with my fingers: pubic hairs, used condoms, lint, crumbs, candy wrappers. Then I cleaned the bathroom, whose toilet contained the worst mixture of shit and vomit I have ever smelled in my life.

When I finally finished, on the verge of passing out the entire time, Phil handed me the sandwich and Diet Coke. "Good job. You're almost a Beta, Big O. You got this." That foot-long meatball sandwich was the best thing I had ever tasted. I savored every morsel like I was an inmate on death row with my final meal. I was ordered back to the basement with my twenty-eight pledge brothers. The lights were off. We were all blindfolded and asked to hold out our right hands. A condom was placed in our hands. Suddenly I was filled with excitement and hope. The prize for enduring all this hell was a gorgeous hot blonde from Delta Gamma. I could just imagine it. This was the best fucking fraternity welcome of all—

Then I heard it.

"*Bahhhhhhhh. Bahhhhhh.*"

A fucking goat.

"Now, who is going first?" one of the members roared.

My dick shriveled in my pants, trying to worm its way back into my stomach.

No no no no no no. . . .

"I said . . . who the FUCK is going first!"

At this point, we were all ready to quit. There was no way in hell I was fucking a goat for this. At a certain point a man has to say enough is enough, and that was goat-fucking for me. In defeat, we started quietly whispering to each other "No way. I'm done."

"This is the ONLY way you can become a brother. Foster! You're up!"

The guy was whimpering as he tore open the condom. They had us all line up in alphabetical order and do the same. Foster unbuttoned his Levi's and pulled them down so he was in his boxers.

"Strap it on!"

As he reached down to put the condom onto his limp dick, the members ripped our blindfolds off and turned on the lights. "Congratulations! You are all now Betas for life!"

My pledge brothers and I started hugging each other like we'd just survived fucking 'Nam. We couldn't believe it. We'd almost just fucked a goat. Now I fully understood the term *brothers for life*.

Being what you could tenuously call "innocent" at the time, moving into that giant frat house destroyed any further notions of my sobriety. And *everyone* was doing cocaine.

I asked one of my brothers one time, as he was snorting lines, "How much do you guys pay for this stuff?"

He said "$100 per gram."

I nearly spit out my cheap beer. "You're kidding."

"Is that a lot?" he asked.

Yes, of fucking course it was a lot. I never did cocaine, but growing up around the Mexican gang "North Side Redondo 13," which was controlled by the Mexican mafia, I'd always heard street talk.

And word on the street was grams of cocaine were sure as shit not being sold for a hundred bucks. A sudden revelation took hold. An opportunity. Not wanting to destroy it, I simply shrugged my shoulders in response. "I don't know, I never bought the stuff." My friend went back to snorting coke, and I sat there exploring the angles of my new epiphany.

These USC kids, especially the frats, powdered their noses just about every night of the week. There were around twenty thousand undergraduates any given year. It was like a small town. And a good percentage of this town liked to party. Goddamn, what if I started buying coke from some of my Mexican gang-member friends from high school on the cheap, then sell it at a premium markup at 200 percent to around $80 a gram, undercutting my competition?

For days, I mulled over the idea. It was stupid. It was ingenious. It was dangerous. But it was safe. Could get me expelled, arrested, hell . . . maybe even killed. But that profit margin was insane. I had no money coming in, because neither of my parents was helping me out with my day-to-day living expenses. I was a poor kid surrounded by the super-rich in an environment where $100 a gram might as well be a quarter in one of those candy machines. I wasn't stupid by any means. And if I was careful and smart about this, maybe I could earn a little extra on the side. Nothing over the top. Buy a new car, take girls out on dates, and actually be able to afford the whole check—it was humiliating that I couldn't. *Fuck it.* I'd at least drop one of my friends a line. This whole thing could just be my imagination, quashed in a moment or in a single sentence uttered by my old pals.

He picked up on the first ring. "Hey, Spanks. Any way we can get ahold of Scrappy?" I asked. Scrappy oversaw all the coke running through Redondo Beach.

I heard him take a drag off his cigarette, as he was just getting off from work. "What do you need?"

"I need to see him in person. Nothing I want to discuss on the phone."

Spanks laughed. "All right. I'll have him call you on his throw-away."

Scrappy called me within twenty minutes. "What's up, college kid? How you liking the University of South Central?"

I laughed it off. He was referring to the fact that USC was in the heart of one of the worst ghettos in LA.

"Real talk, homey. I think I've got an opportunity here. I could sell some of that 'white girl' on campus and be insulated by the fraternity house. It's a safe spot to sell, and I won't have to do anything crazy. Just sit back and make us some paper."

"Oh yeah, youngster, no problem," he said. "I'll drive it up tomorrow afternoon. Let's meet on the corner of Hoover and 28th Street right off the end of Frat Row."

"Frat Row? How do you know about Frat Row?"

"I've driven through there before when meeting the Vatos from 18th Street. Anyway, see you tomorrow. Be there at noon."

And he hung up. I couldn't believe how easy this all was. I stared at the phone as if he'd just offered me a free Ferrari.

The next day, I met him at the corner of my fraternity house off 28th and Hoover. I climbed into the passenger seat of his car. He brought out a Styrofoam takeout container and I thought he was about to hand me a burger and fries; but as he opened it, I saw it was filled with pure white cocaine in plastic baggies. "Wow," I said. I'd never seen that much cocaine before. He took out a scale and handed me the takeout container.

"This is what you got to do," he said. "Weigh it on the scale. Go ahead." I did as instructed. "Now, how much is there?"

"Six ounces," I said.

"Right. This is what I'm gonna do. I'm gonna front them to you at $700 a zip, and there's six of them in here, so you owe me $4,200. This is what you call a 'good faith investment.' You game? I ain't charging you up front. I know money is tight for you up here with all these spoiled kids, and we're homeboys. But I want $4,200 of whatever you make off this. So go see what you can do."

I did the math and decided to sell my coke for $50 a gram, undercutting my competition by 100 percent and with better-quality cocaine. The results were staggering. In just two days I called him back. "Hey, I got your $4,200."

He laughed. "All right, youngster. Ready for a re-up?"

"Yeah . . . hey, by any chance do you have any ecstasy? Anything like that? Maybe some Xanax?"

Some of my buyers had been asking about that. And sure enough, he brought me another Styrofoam container from a hamburger joint, full this time. In it he had eight ounces, three hundred ecstasy pills, and one hundred Xanax.

He said "There you go. See how you do on those."

He gave me real cheap prices. The ecstasy he gave me at $3 apiece and I started selling them at $20. The Xanax he gave me at 50 cents apiece I sold at $5. Pretty soon my margins were so good and so many people wanted my top-tier and cheap coke, I was able to raise the price per gram to $65—still $35 lower than my competition, which were slowly being phased out as my competition altogether.

When I moved into the Beta house, I started using my pledge brother Tommy to sell my drugs. I'd weigh out an ounce of coke, count out one hundred ecstasy pills, and put them in a creatine bottle, as well as fifty xanny bars in a glutamine bottle. I would send Tommy on his way and he would pay me when he ran out. I also conscripted several other guys from other fraternity houses to do the same.

This was easy money. The easiest money I'd ever made in my life, and it just kept pouring in by the bushel. This was how I'd be able to keep up with all the rich kids from Newport Beach and Beverly Hills. How I could go out to the same clubs with them instead of being the pauper stuck back at the fraternity house. All those awkward conversations and little white lies now over and done with: "Hey O, we're going to the 9-0 with a couple Kappas. You in?" "Nah, man. I know it's lame, but I'm stuck doing homework." A total lie. Of course I wanted to be going out to the clubs with them, treating a beautiful girl to some champagne and dancing. I wanted good dinners at those fine dining establishments dotting Santa Monica Beach. The truth was I couldn't afford it. I'd been driving a 1990 Toyota Camry from my grandfather. One of my pledge brothers, his dad was the doctor for the Lakers. My other pledge brother was Dustin Hatfield, whose dad was Bobby Hatfield from the Righteous Brothers. Surrounding me were all these big names and trust-fund kids who'd been spoon-fed their whole lives, driving Denalis, Escalades, AMG Mercedes. And there I was with the 1990 Camry trying to fit in and look somehow attractive or exemplary. This new business changed all that.

Within three months of selling drugs, I was able to purchase a brand-new Mercedes Benz.

"How in hell could you afford this thing?" my dad asked as I climbed out of my Mercedes in front of the house. He traced a finger over the hood along the side, whistling as he went. "Holy shit. You still working at that restaurant over on Santa Monica Boulevard?"

"Sure am," I lied, heading around to the passenger side to let my date out of the car. Truth is, I never worked at a restaurant a day in my life. "Those rich guys give good tips, Pop. And I made some real good investments in the market."

My dad frowned. "The *market?*"

"Stocks and stuff. All my buddies at the fraternity, they got inside info because their folks are flush with cash and know all the top guys on Wall Street. Some of them are major hedge-fund managers and VCs."

"VCs?"

"Venture capitalists, Pop. Anyway, my guys know the good trades and the bad ones. I could help you choose a few if you like. Get you some play money."

Dad waved his hand. "Ain't got no money for that, Owen. You know that. I'm lucky I can afford a steak dinner down at Gino's once a month."

"I mean, I could help set you up, you know . . . give you a few grand to—"

Again, Dad waved his hand, shaking his head. I knew then that the matter was settled. My date, Marianne—a stunning Venezuelan brunette from the Delta Gamma sorority, which was one of my top customers—climbed out of my car in a white Dior dress that clung to her lithe body like Saran wrap, accentuating her curves, her ample breasts, her perfect ass. . . .

"Jesus!" my dad said, his eyes wider than they had been when he saw my ride. "Are you a model?"

Marianne laughed, exposing her perfect white Hollywood smile, and gave a curtsy. "No, sir, I'm not nearly tall enough."

She was right. Even in those Louboutin heels, she barely came up to my chest. She was perfectly throwable, a total firecracker in the bedroom—and out of it. Matter of fact, she blew me on the ride over, me nearly crashing into a family of terrified Chinese tourists right as I climaxed, which would've killed us all at the speed I was driving. Still, I can't really think of a better way to go than that.

My dad reached out his hand and gave his name. He kissed her hand. "What a pleasure to meet you, Marianne. On the way to dinner, you're gonna have to tell me what you see in this bum!"

"Yeah, yeah," I muttered. "Come on, Romeo. You're sitting in the back."

"Nope." My dad shook his head, grabbing the keys from my hand. "I'm driving."

The ride there went as expected, my dad bragging to Marianne about his famous surf buddies, saying one of them remarked one time that he could have gone pro. Then it was back to ancient times when he was a star ballplayer and could have gone pro then too. I didn't mind. I hadn't seen my dad this happy in a long time. He was giving me shit for sure, but in a loving fatherly kind of way.

As we walked through the restaurant inside the Chateau Marmont, one of the top joints in all the city, I thought my dad's eyes would pop out of his head, land on a patron's table, and roll right into their hors d'oeuvres of escargot marinated overnight in chimichurri, slathered in rich French butter, and broiled. He'd never been to a place this nice before. My dad's concept of class was his favorite Italian restaurant, Giovanni's, where he still mostly ate with his hands, a stained napkin firmly embedded in his shirt collar like you see old-timers do. Glancing around the restaurant self-consciously, he quickly tucked his white dress shirt into his pants. "Shit, Owen," he whispered. "If you'd told me where we were going, I'd have brought a blazer."

"Pop. You don't own any blazers."

He sighed. "I'd have bought one."

"Martin," I said to the tuxedoed maître d', a customer who was my liaison now to many of the rich and powerful people frequenting the Chateau, "after you seat us would you mind getting my dad a blazer? Forty-eight L?"

"Not a problem, Mr. Hanson."

Again, my dad frowned. He seemed totally confused, thinking hard about something, but I didn't know what.

It was nighttime, the city lights down below glistening like fireflies in a darkened pasture. Only these lights stretched to the horizon. Martin led us across the courtyard to a beautiful table overlooking all of Los Angeles. He seated Marianne first, then my dad, then me. I quickly slipped a hundred-dollar bill into his hand as I shook it. It was only a moment—a millisecond—but I saw a flash of recognition shine from my dad's eyes. It was then that I knew he realized I wasn't working at any restaurant.

My dad's entire demeanor changed. He didn't seem upset so much as quietly shocked. Where before I couldn't get him to shut up, now it was like I'd just walked in and interrupted him from a dream. He sat watching me in silence while Marianne droned on about her latest trip to Ibiza, where she'd met Kobe Bryant in a nightclub. My dad had an expression that back then I couldn't quite quantify, but now I understand perfectly what it was: he was deeply disappointed, and yet awed.

". . . and I said that's not how I roll," Marianne said, laughing like you do when you tell an uncomfortable joke. "I wasn't going to the *bathroom* with him. Who did he think I was? A *hooker*?"

My dad wasn't listening. He was watching as I arranged my utensils neatly, placing the fine linen napkin over my Armani trousers, arranging everything just so. I had never acted this way in front of him, and I quickly realized this was a dumb move. Too much, too soon. I went from a poor surfer boy wearing only boardshorts to what looked like a businessman in my dad's eyes. This was too grand a gesture, and he wasn't stupid.

"Isn't he married?" I said, trying to get my dad involved in the conversation.

"Yes!" Marianne said. "Isn't that just so gross? Like, I get it, you're Kobe Bryant. But does that mean every pretty girl under the sun is gonna soil her dress in the nasty bathroom of a nightclub?" She scoffed, reaching for her wine glass. "Uh. No thanks."

My dad nodded slowly. In front of him sat a wine glass, but with water. For once in my life, I wished he was drinking. Maybe then he'd be jovial and fun again. Maybe then he would forget. "Son, speaking of the rich and famous . . . you seem to be quite the man here. People know you. Some of them I see turning their heads when you walk by."

I took a large gulp of wine and nervously rubbed my nose; I had snorted a line in the bathroom moments before. I could feel the drug coursing through my tainted veins, making my vision sharper, my energy frenetic, but my mind crystal clear. "Sure, I come here pretty often with one of the fraternity boys. His dad's a producer. They know everybody and everybody knows them. I guess by association some of them are gonna know me too. No?"

Fuck. You idiot. Don't ask leading questions. Ask closed questions. You're in control of this narrative, so fucking think smarter.

My dad chewed his lower lip, an eyebrow slightly raised. "Know you well enough to let you slip a hundred into their hands? That kind of know you?"

"For the jacket, pop. It's just the thing you do. Like a porter at a hotel." Of course it wasn't for the jacket. I'd forgotten to make a reservation because I was too fucked up on a coke- and booze-fueled bender for the past week. I slip Martin hundreds and the reservation magically appears.

"Right," my dad says.

Marianne looked at me, my dad, then back at me. Her frown said *Are you two speaking in code or something?*

"Anyway, how's work going for you, Pop? You keeping real busy as usual?"

My dad didn't respond for a minute. He opened his mouth as if to speak, but thought better of it. He glanced at Marianne. Whatever he'd intended to say, he wasn't going to do it around anyone but me. Suddenly, as if a switch had magically flipped, his demeanor snapped right back to his fun, easygoing self, cracking jokes and carrying the conversation as only a charmer can. But every so often throughout dinner, I would catch him watching me—only snatches, as if recognizing a familiar face in a crowd.

The ride back to my dad's house was quiet. As we pulled up to the curb, I got out of the car to shake his hand. "Thanks for dinner, Owen," he said, then pulled me in close so he could say something quietly in my ear. "You know, I might be old, but I'm not dumb. I know that ain't restaurant money. You don't have to tell your old man; but whatever you're doing, do it safe."

I nodded. "I will, Pop."

He nodded back, taking one last look at me. He let go of my hand. "Safe, Owen."

With that, he walked away.

The more drugs I sold, the more I hung out with the Mexican gang members.

We started going to concerts together, drinking booze, snorting blow. One night I was sitting on Spanky's porch on the North Side drinking beers with a freshly powdered nose, Pennywise music blaring from the souped-up speakers of the '66 Chevy Impala in the driveway, windows rolled down. We sat in the rust-colored glow of a streetlamp, a bright Saturday night, the far-off sound of bottles breaking and men yelling and cursing. Planes tearing through the sky from nearby LAX. Every now and then, someone drove up to the curb, got out, and met with one of the homies. The strangers would slip crumpled bills into their hand and come back with baggies of cocaine.

Big Husky, the top guy in the gang, sat counting bills, a joint dangling from his lips. Tattoos covered his entire body, including "R-13" (Redondo Thirteen) on the back of his left arm and "NSR" (North Side Redondo) on the back of his right. I watched him intently, admiring him. Husky was the top earner in this neighborhood. And he protected it too. Some junkie dealer came on the scene trying to sell narcotics to schoolkids, well, he'd not be around much longer. He'd be found unconscious in the alleys, a broken nose, concussion, bloodied and bruised. This would be his warning. As Husky always said, you only got one warning from him. His next message was lead.

"Husky," I said. He looked at me, eyebrow raised. I touched the back of my arm. "Who jumped you in?" He seemed surprised that I asked. One of the homies—there were five of us—let out a dry chuckle.

"Damn, O! You got some balls on you, *ese*." This was Spanks. "That like askin' a *Heina* her age. You don't go round askin' that shit unless you from the hood or got a death wish."

The others laughed. Husky simply shrugged. "Only people from the neighborhood talk about those things, but let's just say Big Rascal and Chato left me black and blue for three weeks."

I laughed. But this time nobody joined in. Husky stared at me.

"Wait; you serious?"

He nodded, then started talking in Spanish for a minute with the others. Finally he nodded.

"This was back a ways, when some of our rivals from Lawndale started coming over and poisoning our streets, moving in on our turf. It was Chato, Cyclone, Spanks, Smurf, Big Rascal . . . they were not too happy these guys were handing off weed and coke to the youngsters at school and having them deal for them. You had little kids winding up dead cuz they tried the product. You had little kids getting their futures ruined cuz the cops was busting them and not the real guys behind it. Say goodbye to their scholarships, their college. Hell, lot of them just started dropping out of school. One of these kids was my little bro Daniel. Guess you could say it became personal to me.

"Daniel was always good at school. Not like me, no way. Daniel was on the honor roll. Mama didn't roll her eyes when she got his report cards like she did with me. He had teachers singing his praises all damn day, saying he was destined for greatness. Kid could do anything. Hell, I dropped out; but I remember before I did, I kept roping him into doing my book reports and shit, and that shit always got an easy A every damn time. I was proud of my little brother.

"Then one day he got mixed up with these fools. He stopped getting on the honor roll. He stopped showing up to school. I tried talking with him. 'Daniel, *estupido*, what are you thinking? You'll put mom in an early grave from heartbreak. Get your skinny ass to school.' Maybe he listened to me for a week; but a week later, he was back dealing drugs. We went to talk to the gang. We told them they needed to ship the fuck out. No more drugs to the schools. You know what they did? They laughed in Cyclone's face.

"So, I'll tell you what we did. We got one of those mom vans, you know, with the sliding door? We drove through Lawndale and found some of them, opened up the sliding door, and fucking blasted them. And you know what? They stopped selling their drugs on our streets after that. And a few days later, I got jumped in."

A silence fell over us. I looked at Husky, all his tats, his cargo-short pockets stuffed with cash. The casual way he held his beer. Even with a buzz on, his perceptive eyes darted around at anything that looked out of place or suspicious. He was a real bona fide gangster. He lived like a king and was treated like a king. One day, he would die like a king, because that was the rule of the streets. I thought *I could have that. I could be him.*

Taking another sip of beer, I said "I want to do what you do, Husky."

But suddenly, everyone was ditching their beers and standing at attention. Husky was the first to grab his gun. He held it pointed down to the ground. A blacked-out van blaring rap music was slowly driving by, the kind where you can sling open the sliding door and fire a hail of bullets—the same kind Husky had just been talking about. He waited as the van slowed to a stop just in front of the chain-link fence. "Come on, bitch," he muttered. "Make a move."

Because of the tinted windows, I couldn't see who was inside. Everyone stood as still as stone. *Am I gonna fucking die right now?*

The van idled, as if the occupants were weighing the risks of opening that door. But then they hit the accelerator, and the van grumbled away. The tenseness faded, but the caution didn't. "Let's move this inside," Husky said. "Owen, you best get a move on."

"Who were those guys?"

"Don't know, but we're gonna find out. And no, you don't ever want to do what I do. And remember this, Owen. You might be selling our coke and shit, but you ain't one of us. All right? We friends, but you ain't part of my crew and you ain't ever gonna be part of my crew. You're going to get a degree and make something of your life, not fuck it all up."

But I had to ask him one more thing. "Your brother, where's he now? He get his shit together and go back to school?"

Husky shook his head. "No. He's dead."

It was my sophomore year in college when the new volleyball coach looked at me and said "You're too small."

I couldn't believe what I was hearing. The very reason I was *in* college was the *volleyball* scholarship—and this new head coach was eyeing me like I was a six-year-old boy trying to sneak on the big-kid rides at the theme park. I'm SIX-FOOT-FUCKING-THREE, dude. Did this sport magically transition into basketball overnight without my knowing it? The last I checked, sports were about per-formance—and as far as that went, I had a thirty-seven-inch vertical jump with a left-handed whip on me.

He said, "I'm gonna redshirt you this year and work on your vertical jump and tune up your passing in the back row." Redshirt meant he wanted me to take off a year without losing a year of playing eligibility. He went on: "We've got Brook Billings starting opposite hitter and a 6'8" all-American left-hand freshman from Brazil behind him. It's not looking good for you." Brook Billings was an Olympic opposite hitter and would go on to become a Hall of Famer. I couldn't exactly argue there.

Seated in Coach T's office, I bounced my knee off the floor, grip-ping the arms of the chair. "I don't get it," I said slowly, shaking my head. "I wasn't too small last year with Coach Powers here."

He shrugged. "You didn't have me last year. And I'm not Coach Powers."

To him, it was as easy as ordering a cup of coffee at Starbucks.

Yesterday he wanted a macchiato, today he wants a latte. What difference does it make? It's just a perfunctory movement of his lips: an order. There is little meaning or significance in the act. Coach drummed his fingers on his desk impatiently, clearly ready to kick me out of the office because he had more important things to do.

"But I bust my ass out there, Coach," I pleaded. "Come on. Just ask the guys."

"I'm sorry, Owen. You're just not the right candidate."

He inclined his head as if to say "And that's that."

In a last-ditch effort, a crazy thought flashed across my mind: *Wait. Does this guy partake? Maybe I could get him a couple grams of that Peruvian flake on a weekly basis just to sweeten the . . . NO! Don't be fucking stupid, Owen! You'll get your ass expelled.*

Slowly, agonizingly, I stood up from that chair, speechless. But I was *the guy* on campus! If someone needed to score, or if they needed front-row seats at the Lakers' game, the MMA championship fight at Mandalay Bay, or the boxing match in Madison Square Garden, I was the guy! People came to me because they knew I could set them up. I was getting decent grades. I was in the frat. I was six-foot-three, for fuck's sake: Why was I being redshirted?

At the door, I paused, turning around inquisitively. A flash of hope in my eyes. I must have looked like a little kid asking his parents for a toy at the mall.

"Coach T, what if . . . what if I'm just a benchwarmer, you know?" I said it excitedly, quickly, suddenly falling in love with my own idea. Fucking genius! "One of the guys gets injured, I step in to fill his place, you know? Listen, I'll prove myself to you. You don't know how good I can play. I'll show you."

It was a great idea. No harm, no foul. I'll just be a stand-in guy. Humiliating at first, yes, but at some point, I would get an opportunity to show Coach what I'm worth. Hadn't he watched videos from my All-American high school days?

Pursing his lips, Coach simply shrugged again. "Sorry, Owen, my hands are tied."

Oh, fuck off. You're the head coach! But this isn't what I said. I took the lesson in humility, saying, meekly, "Thanks, Coach." What the fuck was I thanking him for? His precious time? The calm ambience of his office? He just redshirted me!

The sound of the door closing behind me would later echo similarly to that of my prison cell slamming shut. With that reverberation of metal is the sound of time passing incredibly slowly and the inevitable emptiness of missed opportunities. The sound that gives you pause, makes you freeze in place wondering if you could have done something more, something different, something better. Like when your wife leaves you during your last fight, slamming the door after saying "I'm not coming back!" You think "Fine, bitch. I don't want you back!" Angrily, you pace the floor of your living room, repeating your frustrations: *She's so stubborn! She never listens to me! She won't try to fix things! All she does is get mad and run away!* You repeat them over and over, playing the film of your marriage in your mind's eye like a reel from a movie. Stubbornly and stupidly, you splice out all the good bits—and there are many—and focus only on the bad shit. The fights, the arguments, the awkward stony silences at public events when something upset you or her. The time you caught her glancing at that guy and you were *convinced* it's because she thought he was good-looking. The way she averts her eyes when she knows she has hurt you.

But once you have exhausted your efforts in remembering all the bad times to fortify your resolve in letting her go, those good spliced bits of film find their way right back where they were. You realize those good times far outweigh the bad. You realize you actually were in the wrong here, and you've just watched the love of your life walk away. But then, she's gone away before. Why don't you just call her like you always do and apologize? You call. The phone doesn't ring. *Disconnected*. She's blocked you. You try again. Again. *Again*. No use. Frantic, you rush out the door into the city streets searching for her, but it's already been ten minutes and now she's nowhere to be found.

Worrisome days spent not hearing from her turn to agonizing weeks. You don't hear from her. Not even when you're served the divorce papers. Surely there's a way to turn back time: all you need to do is convince her you're sorry and it won't happen again. You *are* good enough. You guys can fix this. But it never happens. Your life changed forever when that door closed, and your dumb ass didn't even know it.

Defeated, I left campus, not wanting any of my old teammates or frat brothers to see me. I'm sure they'd heard the news already, and I knew the routine: the clapping on the back, "It's all right, man: just try out again next year." They'd want to get me fucked up and there would be a sense of camaraderie, them saying we've all been there, blah blah blah. I didn't want to hear it. I couldn't bear the embarrassment and the thought that maybe I'm not king shit around here after all. That hole I crawled out of to get here, maybe I should just crawl back into it because that's where I came from, it's where I would return; it's where I belonged.

That day, I drove to South Bay to meet with Spanky and the homies. We drank and got fucked up. They asked me how college was going, when would I become a lawyer so I could get them all out of jail. They referenced that movie *The Sleepers* with Brad Pitt, who was a hotshot lawyer who got his friends off on a murder charge. Brad Pitt's friends had seen the old pedophile who used to abuse them back when they were all at a boys' home. They spotted the guy in a bar many years later, and they promptly shot him in the face.

"When you gonna get some posh job wearing a suit and tie?" they asked me.

Sitting there on the stoop getting all sauced up and coked out, I wondered that myself. What the hell *was* I going to do with my life once this whole college thing was over? I only had two more years and still wasn't set on a major. I'd thought I would have a professional career in sports. That's all I had been working toward my entire life. But now? Now I had to think about real jobs. Real careers. All that shit I never wanted to be part of.

The feeling was one of utter defeat. As the sounds of the guys muted softly behind me and even the screeching roar of airplanes overhead seemed dull and distant, I realized that I felt the same as I did the day my mom had driven off with my little sister all those years ago. That feeling of just not being good enough. Volleyball was something I had worked toward my whole life. I had worked *so* hard to excel at it, just as I had worked so hard to earn the love of my mom. These things in life just happened so goddamn *fast*, you barely had time to take a second and process them. One moment you've got a whole family—your mom cooking dinner every night, and no paper plates, and your sister crawling in next to you with Bunny when she's scared of the monster under her bed—and the next moment they're gone. One moment you have a team—your best friends, the parties, the laughs—and the next moment they're gone too. All the worst events in my life happened suddenly. There was no buildup to them, no warning signs.

"I just want to belong to something . . ." I muttered, then took a huge pull off my beer, instantly regretting the comment. I took a shot of tequila to wash down the shame of it.

"What's that, O?" Spanky said. Good. They hadn't heard me.

"Nothing. I'm just tired."

But the epiphany of that statement was there. It was so damn obvious. I mean, why the hell else would I be here hanging out with a bunch of gangbangers as a white-boy college kid? Obviously it's because I felt I didn't belong at USC. Whenever I felt I didn't belong at USC, I'd go to the South Bay. And whenever I felt I didn't belong with Spanky and his crew, I'd flee back to USC. Sports, the reason I had worked so hard to succeed in them, all went back to that day when I was eight years old and my mom was taking off around the bend, my dad saying "Men don't cry." I wanted to belong to something, and back then it was a family. Now I wanted friendship and camaraderie. This whole drug business was the same shit. I'd never had any intention to become a drug dealer, but the access it gave me, the friends, the admiration I'd never had before, the love—in some fucked-up way, was that why I did all this? In reality, I'd just had an acute identity crisis. Like a human chameleon, I'd just wanted to be wherever it was that gave me a sense of belonging.

Psychoanalyzing myself suddenly made me feel vulnerable, uncomfortable. I took another swig and pushed away the thought. I was over-analyzing, that's all. I ain't a pussy: I'm a man. And getting kicked off the team would give me more time to devote to building this burgeoning drug business. I could leave all that crybaby shit right at the door because that wasn't me. I didn't need validation from anyone.

"So, when you gonna be our lawyer?" Spanky asked again. I think they were actually serious about the whole thing.

"I don't like lawyers," I said. "They're all so full of shit. Tell you what, I'd rather be a drug kingpin."

They laughed. "You just a college boy, O. You can't do what you do on the streets."

"Nah, I won't be the one working the streets. My guys will be doing that for me. I'll be sitting in my mansion up in the Hollywood Hills in a huge office with mahogany furniture and those clocks they have on Wall Street showing all the different time zones, and I'll be on the phone making deals all over the world. And when I'm done for the day, I'll have a gorgeous girl on each arm walking into the best clubs and restaurants in the city. I won't be some low-level pusher. One day, people will know my name. They'll know I'm Owen Fucking Hanson."

A few weeks after Coach T took a raging piss on my parade, I was at the gym doing my normal routine.

I was now getting regular shots of Primobolan and Winstrol from a local bodybuilder in my hometown. I had told him my situation with the coach redshirting me and how I needed to work on becoming a fucking machine so I could get back in the lineup. Didn't matter what position I would be playing or what kind of toxic shit I needed to put into my body to get there.

At the gym I was working out next to Charr Gahagan, the strength and conditioning coach who worked with both the men's volleyball team and the football team. During my workout, he glanced at the veins popping out of my arms every now and then. When I took a break, drinking water and wiping up with a towel, he came over.

"Owen, right?"

"Yeah," I nodded, wiping off my sweaty hand and then reaching it out. He shook it.

"You still doing volleyball?"

"No, Coach T redshirted me. Told me I needed to work on my vertical jump and arm strength."

He looked me up and down. "Well, it looks like you've put on at least twenty-five pounds since I saw you working out on the team last month." I nodded. Little did he know that I was on steroids. "Feel free to stop by the office, and I'll give you some Plyo-box-jump workouts and work on strengthening your rotator cuff."

"I really appreciate that."

"What I remember is you were a damn good player, kid. I saw a few of the preseason matches last year."

The shame. The embarrassment. Creeping up like a slow and sinuous snake. *Fuck it.* "Coach said I was too small." I shrugged. There it was. The truth. "I mean, yeah, I'm the shortest guy on the team at 6'3", but I don't think I'm exactly *small. . . .*" I flexed my arm, veins nearly exploding as if I were Popeye.

Coach scoffed, then eyed me a moment. "You? No. You're not small. But you're wasting your talent and your physique on a sport like volleyball. Maybe instead of trying out all this stuff for volleyball, you should try and join the football team. Ever think of trying out?"

I laughed. "Coach Charr, I've never even caught a football in my life. My folks never let me play in high school because they said it was too dangerous."

The coach shrugged, grabbing his gym bag and heading for the door. "Show up for tryouts, that's all I'm saying. You never know."

For a solid week after that encounter, I thought about his final comment: "You never know." No, clearly you never fucking know, when life can change so drastically quicker than it takes to let out a breath of air. *Fuck it,* I said. What did I have to lose?

When walk-on tryouts happened, I attended along with about fifty other guys, some of them high school all-Americans and junior-college champions, which made things a little intimidating. Tryouts were at the football practice field, and every coach was there—from the head coach, Pete Carroll, to QB coach Steve Sarkisian, offensive coordinator Norm Chow, defensive end coach Ed Orgeron, wide receiver coach Lane Kiffin, tight end coach Brennan Carroll (the son of Pete Carroll), and linebacker coach Ken Norton Jr.

The first round consisted of coordination foot drills, which I'd already been working on for volleyball with Coach Charr. The next drill was a vertical jump test, which I also already had from volleyball, and I managed a thirty-seven-inch vertical jump. Then we had five routes to run with a quarterback coach throwing us the football after each route. It was the first time I had ever been thrown a football, but I still caught three out of five tosses. The final outside drill consisted of the forty-yard dash, which seemed to be the most important. By this time, we had every strength and conditioning coach outside with stopwatches, including Coach Charr. I was the second to last to run it.

I jumped off with an excellent start and finished at 4.65 seconds. Pete Carroll frowned at his stopwatch. The conditioning coach, Jamie, the team's top trainer, said "Hanson, let's do that again. I think we started the clock late." I lined up again, placing my hand down on the grass in the runner's position. I realized I was wearing Nike volleyball shoes while everyone else was wearing football cleats. *Shit, Owen, you blew it man.*

The gunshot sounded and I was off. At the end, I saw Pete Carroll standing with his son, who now had his stopwatch out. They were all sort of frowning at their stopwatches. "4.62," Pete Carroll said. Coach Charr muttered "Holy shit." Suddenly all the coaches were conferring together, whispering. Not thinking anything of it, I grabbed my volleyball backpack and headed to the weight room, where I did the 225-maximum rep on the bench press. I pumped out twenty-five and left the room thinking "Oh, well, if you blew it on that dash, at least you tried."

Two days after tryouts, I heard some of the athletes talking about the almighty "list" coming out—the one that said who had made the team. I was just wrapping up my redshirt volleyball workout—a hundred box jumps and five hundred crunches—when Coach Jackson said "What's this volleyball player still doing here?" referring to me. "Tell him to get up to Coach Carroll's door. There's something he might want to see."

I went up and checked the list, parsing through bodies of athletic hopefuls who were all muttering amongst themselves, seemingly confused. Under the USC football letterhead with the famous Trojan helmet, there was one name, and one name only:

Owen Hanson.

The other guys looked at me like I was some kind of ghost.

No, that can't be right. I ran straight through Heritage Hall to the gym, where I found Coach Charr. "Is that a joke?" I asked. "I was the only name on the list." Charr smiled. Beside him, Coach Jackson answered: "Hanson, see you next week for the start of spring ball. Make sure you go see Tito to get fitted for your equipment and jerseys."

Well, holy fucking shit. I'd made the team.

My first day of football practice I put my shoulder pads on backwards and didn't even think to strap them on. I was so rushed trying to put my jersey over the pads and fit all my leg pads into the proper slots, I showed up to the field like the court jester putting on a knight's armor to elicit laughs from the crowd—all disheveled and looking ridiculous.

The first drill required us to run up and down the field and go through stretches with the conditioning coaches. When Head Coach Carroll showed up, he asked "How's my opposite hitter doing today?"

"Thanks for having me here, Coach. But I'm not sure I have any idea what I'm doing."

He laughed and went about his day.

I quickly realized I was in the tight-end unit, which consisted of Dominique Byrd, Alex Holmes, Fred Davis, Greg Guenther, Nick Vanderboom, and Coach Brennan Carroll. We started with blocking drills on the sled, and I felt like I had two left feet, pushing the sled with everything I had. Then we ran a few five-yard stick routes with Carson Palmer and Matt Leinart—two Heisman Trophy winners—throwing us footballs that felt like rockets. Every finger in my hand felt broken or dislocated.

At the end of practice, we had a scrimmage and they put me up against their number one defense, Kenechi Udeze and Frostee Rucker. Those two had a field day with me, tossing me around like my little sister's old rag doll Bunny. Stunned and a little more than humbled, I was being out-muscled on every single play. I'd go to block, and they'd stick their hands in my pads and toss me ass-over-teakettle like I was just a Q-tip. By the time practice was over and I was in the locker room taking off my jersey as if it weighed a thousand pounds, half the defensive linemen were cracking jokes about me.

One of them finally said "Listen, man, you got your shoulder pads on backwards and you forgot to strap up."

Oh, great. Didn't think to tell me that before practice though, huh?

Backup quarterback Matt Cassel fired back: "What do you expect, fellas? This guy hasn't played football in his life. This is literally his first day. How well did you guys do on your first day, back when you were eight years old? As good as Owen during tryouts?" The guys all exchanged confused glances. They fell silent. "Yeah. Didn't think so."

A routine started falling into place. A strange one, but a routine nonetheless.

At the crack of dawn, I'd wake and get ready for school, then bag up twenty to forty grams of cocaine in little gram baggies alongside fifty pills of ecstasy, which I kept in a jar in my sock drawer. My frat brother Tommy was one of my dealers; he knew the drill: for every twenty grams he sold, he got a gram. For every fifty pills of E, he got two pills. Being that his stock ran dry at some point every day, he was making out with a decent little score. Out of caution, he would only sell to our fraternity and several sororities. People would come to our room on the second floor of Beta. We lived in a little protected bubble, as only the Betas knew the password to enter the building.

By 6:30 a.m. I was in the weight room training for football, then on to class: Public Policy, Business Management. After school it was football practice. At 2:00 p.m. we'd be watching old football reels. Learning the plays: the pros, the cons, the mistakes and victories. By 4:00 we were out on the field practicing until 7:00, at which point we went to the training table, all 115 of us, and ate like kings, scarfing down all the proteins and carbs we needed. By 8:00 p.m. I was back at the fraternity house, Tommy sitting at his desk with white powder under his nose while slugging a cocktail. Several lines of coke were neatly laid out beside his computer mouse, and in front of him the computer screen showed he was typing up a history essay. His fingers struck that keyboard like lightning strikes.

Tommy spun around in his office chair a bit too quickly, catching me by surprise. Especially with that manic *"Herrrrrrre's Johnny!"* on his crazy-ass face. "O," he said quickly, sniffling, "we're all sold out man all done fucking zero bro gone."

"All right. Chill." I went to the sock drawer and started grabbing baggies. "You know if you do too much of that stuff, it's not gonna do your history paper any damn bit of good."

"Ha!" he said.

I started weighing more coke. "Let's do another fifty grams . . . and another hundred pills. Are you partying tonight?"

He laughed maniacally, his eyes bulging. The frat-boy version of Nicholas Cage. "It's Friday night bro, of course I'm partying. What are you, nuts?"

I'd hand him the goods and he'd go out and party—sometimes I'd join—and by midnight, the drugs were all gone and my pockets were stuffed with several thousand dollars in cash. This all sounds great, but the truth was I didn't know what the fuck I was doing, really. I mean, my drugs were kept in my *sock drawer*. I wasn't some sophisticated drug dealer at the time. I was just trying to make money and keep up the racket. I wasn't organized; hell, at first I didn't even know how to work the scale. I didn't know salesmanship lingo. My rule was that the product would sell itself. I'd always tell people "I don't cut it with baby laxatives like the Mexican dealer down at the corner gas station." My policy was: Try a line, and if you don't like it, don't buy it. And for the E pills, I'd say "If you don't roll your ass off on these, I'll refund your money come Monday." Simple. Back then, I was just in it to make money and keep up with the Joneses, and in this case the Joneses were basically the entire USC campus: I had a lot of keeping up to do.

Friday and Saturday nights were mostly a fantastic blur of drug-and-sex-fueled mayhem. At the Beta house, we always had kegs and a full bar on the weekends. Our parties started after hours, around 2 a.m. once the school bar, the 901 Club, closed. Tommy and I would have two sorority girls in our room, and I'd be passing out ecstasy like Tic-Tacs, sipping GHB like a fine, smooth whiskey.

Come sunup, our beds would look like the dirty sweat-stained leftovers of a crazy 1970s porn shoot. By noon, the Kappa girls would be walking out of the Beta house in the infamous Beta Walk of Shame. They would stop at our kitchen on the way out, where our cook Hector would supply them with two Hector McMuffins. He would always give the sorority girls Hector McMuffins after a party. That was the weekend routine.

Sunday mornings, I was always getting breakfast with my old pal Spanky, my initial hookup to the guys that started selling me drugs. He was your typical Southside Mexican gang member, "R-13" tatted on his arms, one of which had a full sleeve. His head was shaved, so smooth that it glinted with the sunlight pouring in through the diner's windows. He wore baggy Dickies khaki pants and Chuck Taylors and a crisp white T-shirt that was three sizes too big for him.

When I met him, I'd be coming down from forty-eight hours of coke and booze and rolling my ass on E and Molly. One Sunday, leaning over the breakfast table with a coffee mug shaking in both hands from all the drugs and lack of sleep—the coffee inside vibrating like mud puddles from *Jurassic Park* whenever the T-Rex came lurking—I brought the coffee to my lips and spilled half of it on the table. "Ah, shit." I mopped it up quickly with a pile of napkins, ran out of them, and said, "Waiter, more napkins please?"

Spanky eyed me judgmentally.

"What?" I said through a mouthful of coffee, offended. "It's just a little bit of coffee. Did I get any on you?"

All Spanky did was shake his head.

When the waiter arrived, I ordered two plates of Huevos Rancheros, half a dozen hard-boiled eggs, toast, two sides of bacon, a large glass of orange juice, and a pitcher of Bloody Marys. Spanky and I made small talk until the food arrived, then I dove in and devoured it all in five minutes. Leaning back, I let out a nice loud belch and felt like at last there was a God, and God was good because my hangover would now likely be gone by noon. Especially with that second pitcher of Bloody Marys in front of me, staring at me obsequiously like the Holy Grail glinting in firelight from across a tomb.

I poured myself a glass and took a large gulp, letting out an obnoxious sigh. "That's good shit," I said, sitting back with a dumb smile on my lips. Again, Spanky simply stared. I could piece together why: dotting my shirtsleeve like a Jackson Pollock painting were speckles of dark maroon blood, a whole mess of it, from a fight I'd broken up at the frat house the night before. I was just trying to help, getting right in the middle of it, but one guy got a final right hook in and then blood spurted all over my favorite dress shirt. On the side of my collar there may have been a little bit of puke; I mean, I let it all out over the railing and just wiped my lips with the collar. I know it's gross, but I was fucked up and we didn't exactly have warm towels on hand. My elbows were bruised from God knows what, and I probably smelled like the sidewalks of Skid Row on a sweltering summer afternoon—all the piss and shit and puke and blood. It's fine. It was just an ordinary weekend.

"What are you staring at me for?" I asked.

Spanky looked at me forlornly like I was some kid lost at the amusement park. He took a careful sip of his Bloody. I found it ironic, the look he was giving me: a gang member judging the frat boy. It felt slightly sobering for a moment. Only for a moment.

"You sure you want to be going down this path, man?" he asked.

I scoffed and took another drink. "What path?"

He was shaking his head. "You're hung over, but you're no fool, O."

I shrugged. Took another drink. That shit went down *smooth*.

"You're going to school at probably the best college in the country right now."

"Yeah," I said proudly. "We were College of the Year."

"Right, and you got so much going for you. You got your grades, you got the football shit now, you got the degrees coming your way. You sure you want to do everything you can to fuck it all up?"

That wounded me. Hurt a little. Spanky was my friend. Suddenly I felt guilty because here I was, some white dude from a blue-collar family, and I was given the golden ticket; the ticket Spanky probably only dreamed of getting before he realized his race and his background and the streets prevented him from ever having such a ticket, and therefore he'd have to find other means to get it. But those means meant prison, murder, death. There was no college degree at the end of that path, no classic family, no home with a white picket fence and a Golden Retriever loping in the yard. For Spanky there was no American Dream, and here I was, squandering my own.

"It's just for the school years," I said. "Come on, Spanks; you know me, dude. I don't have any money of my own. My folks don't have money either. I just gotta keep going until school is over so I can hang while I'm here. It's tough to survive with all these rich kids around and all their 'fuck you' money from mom and dad. I don't have that. I'm one of the only fraternity brothers who doesn't carry around an American Express black card. Dude, I'm the son of a construction worker."

Spanky said, "My dad is still in Jalisco. You know what he does? He farms seven days a week, 365 days a year, still never making enough money to come to the States and see us, as his only goal in life is to work to support his family."

My face reddened. "I get your point," I said quietly.

"O, you don't need all that money to pay for school, and you don't need all that money to have fun. How much you making right now?"

"Two or three grand a week. Five grand during Rush Week."

"So you're clearing over $60k a year."

I nodded.

"That ain't bad for a twenty-year-old doing football and school full-time. You really need all that? Need to be taking such big risks that could throw your whole college career down the drain?"

"My whole life I've been living on handouts. I don't want to be doing that anymore."

Spanky leaned in. "All's I'm saying, O, is there comes a time when a man needs to know his limits."

One might find this ironic, but my first trip to Tijuana was not to buy hard drugs, but to buy horse drugs.

Being one of the smaller guys on the tight-end squad meant I had to start putting on some weight. So I went down to a veterinarian clinic in Tijuana that was recommended to me. As I reached the door, several Caucasian bodybuilders piled out, definitely American.

This is the right spot.

I went up to the girl sitting at the desk and said, "*Buenos dias, señora. Necesito comprar asteroids.*" (Good day, ma'am. I need to buy steroids).

"I speak English," she said.

"Okay, in that case I need some performance-enhancing drugs, please."

If I did this in America, I'd get a phone call straight to the police. But this was Mexico. So, the girl simply took the phone off the receiver and buzzed one of the veterinarians. She spoke a few lines and then waved me to a door behind her. "Last room at the end of the hall," she said.

I headed down the hallway, peering into rooms as I went. I saw dogs, cats, and pet rabbits. Then at the end of the hall the door opened to reveal a middle-aged brunette woman in scrubs. She gave me a big smile. "Come on in."

I explained my situation, and she took notes. When I was done, she went to a pair of locked cabinets, unlocked them, and grabbed boxes of drugs. She set them down in front of me. "These are common steroids for your needs: Trenbolone, Sustanon 250, and Winstrol. There is a very specific regimen to follow. I know a lot of you guys don't like to follow rules, so you end up *overdoing* it, which threatens your health and in fact makes you more susceptible to long-lasting and even irreversible damage. Kidney failure, liver tumors, early heart attacks, stroke. This is nothing to mess around with."

"I'll be responsible with them," I lied.

She handed me three vials of each, which was a twelve-week cycle—just enough to get me prepared for summer training camp and then get off and shed them from my system in time for the NCAA drug tests. I paid her four hundred dollars. I'd noticed some medical tape by the sink in her office. "Can I borrow some of that?"

I went to the bathroom and dropped my pants, taking out the tape and taping the vials of drugs to my legs. Then I slipped Nike compressor shorts over them, and my pants. You couldn't even see any bulges.

An hour later, I was at the border. I stopped my truck as a stern Border Patrol officer came around to my window. The sudden rush was electrifying. It felt like the first time that I'd done coke. But my hands were steady on the steering wheel, my demeanor cool and confident.

"You bringing anything back with you?" he asked, examining the bed of the truck, which was empty.

"No, sir. I was just visiting my girlfriend for the weekend."

The vials of drugs felt cool against my legs. I could feel the liquid sloshing around in them as I gently bounced my foot.

The officer nodded. "All right, you're free to go."

It's stupid, but this experience would serve as a launch period for my brashness in dealing drugs. It was That. Fucking. Easy. Not like I had kilos of powder stashed in the wheel wells—at least, not yet—it was just a couple hundred dollars of steroids, and I doubt they would have even booked me for it. They probably would have just confiscated them. But this adrenaline rush from being so close to getting caught but not—it would become incredibly addictive.

Driving back to campus, I felt like I'd just duped the goddamn FBI. I was untouchable. And if I could get some steroids across the border so easily, weren't there ways I could get coke? As I drove, I reached down and pulled the taped vials off my legs. My leg hair came off with the tape and it hurt like fucking hell, but I didn't care. It was worth the cost of admission.

Still, I was carrying around illegal drugs and I'm not a dumbass, so I put the stuff into a subwoofer speaker that I had in the back seat until I got back to campus. Then they went from my speaker to my backpack and on into the sock drawer, which now had half a kilo of cocaine and a few thousand pills on the regular. I was running out of room for my socks.

Now I had to start taking the steroids. I'd buy syringes online from a medical site called GetPinz.com. At the time I weighed in at 210, but my coaches were telling me I should be a solid 240. Within a month of adjusting my diet to be high-caloric as well as taking the steroids and doing weight training, I had reached that 240. And I was no longer the green kid: I had earned the respect of my teammates because they saw I was willing to work harder than anyone else.

Around this time, my confidence in dealing was building up. My pledge brothers and I had a trip to Cabo San Lucas planned, and we all knew firsthand that Mexican drugs were shit. You'd have to get them from some grungy stinky little guy on the street corners and never knew what the drugs were cut with or how they had been produced. You could even get caught with a bag full of vitamin supplements or baking soda that you just spent several hundred bucks on. We didn't want to run the risk of getting bad drugs, so instead, I ran the risk of smuggling three hundred ecstasy pills and an ounce of blow onto the plane.

The compression shorts were back.

Before we all went to LAX, I strapped all three hundred pills into the liner of my compression shorts, right on the edge of my ass crack. The blow I taped underneath my balls. Walking through security, I thought I was going to pass out from the adrenaline and fear. I had nearly a decade-long jail sentence taped beneath my nut sack. What would happen if they found out? Would they tackle my ass? Taze me? Cuff me right there in front of everybody? With a little bit of steroids, I'm sure it wouldn't be that big a deal. But this was a whole lot more. And I fucking *loved* it.

I passed through security like a champ, my brothers eyeing me covertly along the way, all probably thinking I'd be in a Mexican prison before they even checked into the hotel. It wasn't Security I was concerned with; it was Customs.

We got off the plane and were walking through a packed Customs. They had this big sign that said *Pase* and *Alto*, which meant "Pass" and "Stop." Below the sign and attached to the pole was a button you had to press, which would then indicate either green for Go or red for Stop.

What the fuck is this?

I tapped the fraternity brother in front of me, Hatfield. "Bro, what the fuck is that thing?"

Hatfield shook his head. "I'm just as confused as you."

"How does it decide who stays or goes?"

"It's probably random, on a computer. Probably every ten or fifteen people who get green, some random guy gets red." Suddenly, he got it. His eyes widened. They passed down to my board shorts. He said "Oh, fuck. . . ."

Now I was sweating bullets. I knew my luck couldn't go on forever. Maybe I could sneak steroids past a lazy Border Patrol agent, but this was completely randomized. This was a machine. If my luck was now down to technology, I was fucked. I barely even understood computers.

A guy hit the button and the red light came on with a buzzer. He was taken out of the line and patted down. He stood there casually. They felt his arms, his sides, his legs. Then they let him pass.

Fuckfuckfuckfuckfuck.

The guys were looking at me, scared. I counted the bodies between me and that godforsaken button. Nineteen people. Jesus Christ. I was number twenty! My mind was racing, trying to think of an exit strategy but coming up blank. There was no way I could ask someone to swap places in line, it would be extremely obvious and would raise red flags. I literally was being corralled like cattle to this damn thing. No going back, only forward to the bolt pistol.

Beads of sweat formed on my eyebrows and trickled down my nose. I kept wiping it away, but it would come right back. My hand was shaking. What if I faked a medical emergency? No, too suspicious. Could I pretend that I'm about to piss myself so I could run to the bathroom? I looked around the huge Customs rooms; no bathrooms. They must do that by design so they can trap people from flushing drugs down the toilet just like I would be doing if I could. No. My only option was the bolt pistol.

Fifteen people in front of me. Ten. Eight. I kept praying for that red light to go off before I got to it but it didn't happen. Six people left. Three. One.

Time slowed to a murmur as I stared at that goddamn button. The sound it made on red reminded me eerily of the buzzer that sounded in those prison films when they did roll call and the cell doors all opened. How ironic. This was my prison sentence.

All my brothers' eyes were now glued to me. They watched in trepidation as I slowly reached my hand forward, covered in sweat. My index finger extended, slowly reaching the hard plastic of my impending doom. I took a deep breath.

I pressed the button.

The light flashed green. I had to blink several times just to confirm that I wasn't in some distorted reality, a Twilight Zone teasing me with a false color when it was actually red and there were guys coming to frisk me and find my drugs. But no, it was green. I could have fallen to the floor and wept.

As the customs official was stamping my passport, I looked back at the fraternity brother behind me. He pressed the button:

RED.

Sitting on the beach with the sand sifting between my toes, I watched with amusement all the little Mexican dealers approaching tourists with their shitty cocaine. One of our guys, who didn't know I had all the coke with me, purchased a little dime baggy from these people. He sat smiling after his purchase, watching the waves, his whole demeanor saying "This is it." Then he dipped his pinky into the bag and brought up a little to his nose and snorted. "Fuck!" he shouted.

"What's the matter?" I called over.

He wriggled his nose, frowning. "It's goddamn baking soda! That shit burns!"

We all laughed.

"Don't worry, bud, I got the real stuff back at the hotel."

Later, when we were done with the beach, I bagged up all the cocaine I had brought. It ended up being fifty-six half-gram baggies. Hatfield laughed as I showed him the stash. "You crazy mother-fucker, O. Usually folks bring cocaine *from* Mexico, not into it."

Hatfield was not wrong. But at that time, I didn't have any cartel associations; I was just working with the street gangs out of L.A. The cartels were busy though. Starting in the 1980s, a kilo of cocaine might cost $1,000 to refine and about $4,000 to smuggle into Mi-ami, where Pablo Escobar's guys would turn around and sell it for $50,000 to $70,000 a kilo. It was around $30,000 per kilo today, but it cost more the farther it had to be smuggled. Southern Califor-nia, Texas, and Miami were the cocaine capitals of the U.S., but over in New York and Canada you could earn sixty-five percent more than what the wholesale price was in the Southern states, sometimes more than $50k per kilo. I wondered what it would be like to tap into those markets. Better yet, there were places that cocaine was virtually non-existent because of difficult supply routes—how much did it cost per kilo there? Double the wholesale price? Triple? My mind drifted to faraway places like Europe and Australia. Maybe one day I would find out firsthand.

After bagging up the coke, I joined my pledge brothers down at the sprawling hotel bar, which filtered out onto the beach. Every-body was buying me drinks because they knew I was about to show them the best spring break of their lives. We went to the famous "Office" bar and then on to Mango Deck on the beach slugging drinks and snorting coke all night. Eventually I met my future full-back and best friend Brandon Hancock, a.k.a. "Swolecock." He was sitting beachside with his pops drinking ice-cold Modelo, all lubed up in tanning oil, the sun reflecting off him like a mirror. I watched as USC girls came up to him left and right, as everyone had already heard he was about to be the star fullback. At seventeen years old, Brandon had skipped his senior year of high school and was the top recruit. He was 240 pounds and had a six-pack I hadn't seen on any of the college guys. The dude was jacked. He had started bodybuilding at thirteen and his more well-known nickname, understandably, was "The Hulk." I introduced myself, saying I'd heard he was going to join our team and why didn't he come with me as I was heading to the famed Squid Roe. "I'll show you how we party at USC," I said.

"All right, man."

By the time we got to Squid Roe, Brandon was shirtless and had two Penthouse twins rubbing on him, one on each side, sandwiching him. They danced to Reggaeton music and took tequila shots from each other's mouths. I threw disco biscuits in all three of their mouths to keep the party going. With his physique and his confidence, you'd have thought Brandon was a twenty-three-year-old *Health and Fitness* model, not a seventeen-year-old kid. Pretty soon we were up on the fourth floor, Brandon and the twins groping each other unabashedly like they were prepping for a threesome, and the whole club was rolling on my ecstasy. Everyone was having the time of their lives, all because of the drugs I'd carried through customs between my ass cheeks and under my balls.

Seated at the bar watching my pledge brothers dance with gorgeous girls, dozens of people all rolling in the club off my drugs, I felt a profound sense of accomplishment. Sounds ridiculous, I know, but being a blue-collar kid growing up in a modest beach bungalow without two quarters to scrape together, the feeling was one of euphoric pride. *I did this,* I kept saying to myself. All these people were having a blast because of me. That strange sensation was more addictive than the coke I'd been producing. People looked up to me as the guy who could get them whatever they wanted. I didn't have to, but I did it because of that same sense of belonging. I felt at peace here like I never had before. People knew my name not because it was attached to some famous person, like so many of the other guys—and those were the guys who got everything in life. I wasn't some douche whose dad was so-and-so in Hollywood or Silicon Valley, a guy whose very name commanded respect and awe. It was not forced like that. People knew my name simply because I provided for them, and they liked me.

Under the flashing blue neon lights and the dancers in birdcages suspended from the ceiling, I met Katrina M., daughter of the legendary owner of one of America's top surfing brands. Eventually Brandon, the twins, Katrina, and some USC students decided to head to Brandon's dad's house in Pedregal—the most famous gated community in Cabo—right next to Sammy Hagar's place. We ended up turning the place into a full-blown orgy. Brandon hooked up with the Penthouse twins, my boys Hats and Mike were hooking up with girls they'd brought back from Squid Roe. People were fucking in the jacuzzi, the pool, on the deck, and on the beach— which Katrina and I were guilty of. It was the best sex of my life.

Everyone felt amazing, especially me. I was Dr. Feelgood, prescribing everybody a good time with Molly, ecstasy, and bumps of coke throughout the night. They would come up to me with open mouths and I'd toss a pill in. Playing the roles of a glorified concierge and a party planner, it seemed I had found my calling. I was bringing all these people together in an event that they would never forget. It made me happy to see them happy. Made me content because at long last I was fulfilling some sense of purpose that I'd always lacked, even if it was hedonistic and illegal and fucking crazy.

I realized that not only were these people having the time of their lives, they were also willing to pay anything to enjoy that feeling again and again. Kids all across the university now knew me as the one guy who could make that happen. Whether it was on campus, in Cabo, Costa Rica, Europe, or Newport—I would continue to make it happen. This was my calling in life.

And I was going to see it through.

I felt like the titular character in the film *Rudy*, which I grew up admiring. Maybe I was too small, and maybe I never scored a touchdown or made a game-defying play, but every single day I gave it my all on the football field.

Though I was a bit of a laughingstock on my first day at practice, I had now earned the respect of my teammates through my hard work and insatiable determination. The best guys performed better than me, but no one worked as hard as me. I never once missed practice, not even when I was sick as a dog with the flu and the simple act of standing sent electric shockwaves through my nauseated head. I never missed a volunteer workout in the summer. I would often throw up after practice because I had worked so hard, rinsing the vomit from my mouth at the sink like blood wiped from a fighter's face—the feeling of sickness and pain transitioning to one of mild euphoria.

The environment was even more closely knit than my actual fraternity house, where so much of the social activity and community functions revolved around drugs and booze. Maybe it's ironic, given that I was the biggest black-market concierge on campus and a frat bro, but to a degree, I found myself getting tired of all that. Where before my community derived from the drug-and-sex-fueled parties at my fraternity house, now I largely called my team home. We were a brotherhood forged in iron and sweat, each win and loss bringing us closer together, no matter the stakes. The sense of belonging since I'd come to college now amplified, I found myself wishing it would last forever, that there would be no graduation in the spring, and I could stay here and continue like some of my fifth-year frat brothers who were so addicted to campus life that they paid little attention to their grades and had to keep staying back. While my friends and teammates kept talking about what comes next—the NFL, law school—I was too content to even look past the present moment. I didn't want to know what lay around the corner: I just wanted to be around my team, my family on the field.

Our last game against UCLA, I was made captain by Coach Carroll because of how well I had done in practice that week. UCLA was our arch-nemesis, our ultimate cross-town rival. This was an honor like none else. Legends Matt Cassel, Reggie Bush, Matt Leinart, and I walked out onto that field hand in hand, bathed in the bright lights and the crowd's thundering roar. We met at the fifty-yard line with the four UCLA captains and the refs and shook hands, letting UCLA choose tails on the coin toss. They won the toss, but we won the game—29–24.

My hard work eventually netted me a spot on the 'Gladiator of the Coliseum' poster, awarded by strength and conditioning coaches to fifty of the toughest players attending practice and workouts over the summer. The photo was taken in front of Heritage Hall, me flexing shirtless alongside my teammates, many of whom would become All-Americans and future NFL draft picks. The poster was sold at the campus bookstore, at concession and merchandise stands at the Coliseum, and online. Then the NCAA Madden video game came out on PlayStation, and I was on that too. I'd get drunken calls from friends back home saying, to the tune of clinking glasses and bong rips and laughter, "BRO! We're playing YOU on Madden right now!" "I'm playing your character—jersey number eighty-eight!"

Because there was no NFL team in Los Angeles at that time, we the Trojans were viewed as the closest thing to it. When we won our first national championship, we were the talk of the town. When we won the second at the Orange Bowl in Florida, we were suddenly legends. The Miami Dolphins were last place in the NFL, and everybody kept clamoring for us to play against them, as we would have beat an NFL team. We had the keys to the city, whether in Hollywood enjoying customary bottle service at the hottest club— where we were always bumped to the front of the line, taken to a table, and comped drinks all night—or at restaurants where a quick glance at our championship rings instantly netted us VIP tables in the back without even having reservations. We were Los Angeles's golden boys of sports. And the golden opportunities seemed like they would never run dry.

One night Matt Leinart, Heisman trophy winner and future backup quarterback for Kurt Warner, took Brandon Hancock and me to a new nightclub called Club LAX. The club's VIP host took us to the best table, right next to the DJ booth. Six bottle-service girls served us bottles of Grey Goose in whatever cocktail we wanted. Another time, my girlfriend's dad called me; he was the head of Quiksilver, and he invited me down to tour the company with Matt Leinart. "Do you think you could get me a signed football from him?" he asked. Of course I could. Matt and I were picked up by a chauffeur and taken to the factory, where Matt signed a football and both of us went on a $1,000 shopping spree courtesy of the CEO.

These were all the accoutrements of being a modern-day celebrity, and the feeling was intoxicating. But even more than the materialistic angle of it, there was true meaning. One of my favorite things was going to the hospitals to take pictures with kids who had cancer.

These little guys had four, maybe five months to live, and one of the things they wanted most before they passed was a signed glove or a ball or simply a picture with one of the "Gladiators." Their smiles were huge, and whenever I'd see one, I couldn't help but smile myself. It was better than signing autographs or jogging out from the Coliseum tunnel at game time. On those occasions with the kids, I would have this sense of all-around joy that confirmed "This is what you were meant to do with your life. This is where you belong." During a game, I recognized one of the kids from the hospital. I kept telling myself that come the conclusion of the game, I was going to make sure that boy got my custom Nike gloves. All four quarters I made sure to keep an eye on him and exactly where he was sitting— right on the fifty-yard line, two rows up. When the game ended, he moved toward the tunnel, and I just ran like a bat out of hell bee-lining it right for him with my gloves. I handed them to him, and I will never forget the smile on that boy's face.

Other times at the hospital with Brandon and Frostee Rucker, our huge defensive end, we'd show up and all the kids would come running to us. They would jump up and hug us like we'd known them all their lives. I had a Trojans T-shirt that I got my entire team to sign for one of the boys at the hospital. The size-small shirt barely fit around my arm, but it hung loosely on this kid like a dress. I looked at him with a strange amalgamation of joy and fear; joy because it made him so happy, it was infectious; fear because I couldn't help but wonder if he would still be around to wear it come next season.

The 2004 Rose Bowl was my first taste of epic football: the USC Trojans versus the Michigan Wolverines. It was January, with a biting chill in the air, but my adrenaline was so high that the winter air might as well have been steam from a sauna. I could have played in my fucking jockstrap. The air was electric with the promise of success. If we won this game, we would most likely become national champions. And win we did: 28–14.

The AP Press named us "National Champions," and LSU also earned a piece of the title with the #1 rank through the Bowl Championship Series (BCS) poll. It was the first time in college history that two teams split the #1 title, earning us both a visit to the White House. At the end of that game, the crowd was tossing thousands of red roses onto the field. I picked one up and put it between my teeth, taking photos with my team. Right after our win, I was one of a handful of guys invited by Hugh Hefner to the Playboy Mansion, touring through the place with all its pets: the signature Playboy Bunnies but also the exotic animals like monkeys, cockatoos, peacocks, pelicans, and African cranes. I felt like I had slipped into a dream after our championship win at the Pasadena Rose Bowl and woken up in this sex-charged wonderland of infinite desire. We partied until four in the morning doing coke, ecstasy, drinking. We didn't do anything crazy, but we didn't have to: simply the honor of being invited was enough.

Coach Carroll was always setting up the coolest shit for our team. On Mondays we would watch a film from our previous Saturday's game. One Monday, the lights turned out in the meeting room and all 110 of us looked around at each other, confused. Then we heard it—"Drop it like it's hot, drop it like it's hot. . . ." The next thing we knew, the lights came back on, and Snoop Dogg was coming down the center aisle with a shirtless Coach Carroll in tow, Snoop with the mic in his hand rapping that immortal classic and finishing off with a huge chest bump with Coach. Then Coach said into the mic: "Hey, guys, listen, I'm going to have Snoop dress up today and join us in practice." Snoop put on full pads, helmet, and practice jersey and played with us like it was any ordinary Monday.

I wasn't one of the top guys. I had walked out onto the field for tryouts and gotten a spot without having played football a day in my life. Simply being a part of the team was a huge accomplishment. Still, getting pummeled day in and day out during practice, I couldn't help but wonder how good I would be if I *had* been practicing all my life. I was going against the number one defense of USC every day and getting thrown around like a rag doll, stitches on my chin, concussions. I was tough cannon fodder. Sometimes I'd ask myself, *Is that all I am?*

I got my answer during the final quarter in a game against the Washington Huskies. When my tight end coach called me up, I thought he must've found my drug stash and taken the whole goddamn thing. I pointed at myself, perplexed. "Wait, *Me?*"

"Owen, get your ass in there!"

I got in with two minutes left on the clock. Coach put me in for a blocking play. As if in slow motion, I executed the block against my guy, and we got the first down. And right then I knew the game was over. We were two touchdowns ahead, and now all we had to do was take a knee and run out the clock, which is exactly what we did. That season we were undefeated, 14–0, and we went on to play the Orange Bowl in Florida, defeating the Oklahoma Sooners 55–19 and winning our second championship in as many years. Over those two years, our record was now 27–1.

During the after party, Coach Carroll said "None of you motherfuckers better be falling asleep tonight. We're partying until the private plane picks us up."

We did party all night, but I couldn't help falling asleep. Coach came into my room at nine in the morning: "Hanson, what the fuck are you doing, man? I told you, you got to stay up!"

I was toast. Worst hangover of my life. "I'm sorry Coach," I said,

"I couldn't help it."

He chuckled. "Go on. You're gonna miss the plane."

When I boarded, all my teammates were laughing. Here I was O-Dog, Master of Libations, Mr. Party, Doctor O-Dog with my litany of PEDs and seemingly bottomless sock drawer of drugs, and I was the only guy on the team who passed out and nearly missed the plane.

All I could do was smile.

Pretty soon my reputation was expanding beyond the Heritage Hall of USC. I was quietly making a name for myself in the dark annals of private country clubs, fraternities, college and professional sports circles, and other wealthy and influential cliques.

For me, my drug dealing was becoming a master class in networking as I was thrust into a veritable who's-who of the sports, business, and entertainment world. Down the line, if I got caught speeding along the Santa Monica Freeway with a stash of coke in my subwoofer, I'd pull out my driver's license with head L.A. Sheriff Leroy Baca's business card taped not-so-discreetly to the back. He was a huge USC fan and donor, and around town there was a saying called "Friends with Leroy," which meant if you flashed his business card, you got off.

Maybe I needed a whole shitload of cash for a large shipment of cocaine that came dirt-cheap because the original buyers had gotten arrested in a sting and my people now had to move the product fast: I could ask for a one-month loan with 20 percent interest from Lou Ferrigno Jr., the movie star's kid who would front it to me no questions asked. Of course, I'd make thirty grand off that loan in about a week.

Or maybe it had nothing to do with money or power but was

simply romantic in nature. I meet a girl who's a huge Lakers fan and loves Kobe Bryant. I'd text my pledge brother Luke Lombardo, whose dad was the Lakers' doctor, and before I knew it, I'd have two seats right behind the Lakers' bench with my date meeting Kobe before the game. She would fuck my brains out that night, probably juxtaposing Kobe's face onto mine, but she would fuck my brains out nonetheless.

I saw the potential of these powerful connections and mined them mercilessly. Star athletes from rival colleges were now hitting me up to help amp up their game. These were kids who had an actual chance of getting into the NFL. My job was to provide them with the necessary performance-enhancing drugs (PEDs) to become faster and stronger for the Combine Test, the NFL's official test held at Lucas Oil Stadium in Indianapolis every year. Only the top 1 percent of NCAA Division 1 athletes are invited. The test consists of a forty-yard-dash, bench press of 225 pounds, vertical jump, and cone drills. It was the biggest deal in college football, so obviously my guys needed to be in the best shape of their lives.

With a little research, I was able to identify their specific needs and how to address them. For strength, I would prescribe Sustanon-250, Trenbolone, and Cypionate. For gaining muscle mass and weight, Anadrol, Dbol tablets, and Deca or Nandrolone. For endurance it was always Winstrol, human growth hormones (HGH), and Anavar. One of the most famous linebackers at USC asked for HGH so he could stay healthy during the off-season. I got him those, and he'd later be inducted into the NFL Hall of Fame just like a lot of the players who came to me. Even MLB players started coming to me, some of whom were famous closers of the World Series, and future UFC champions.

I trained these guys on how to load the syringe, which consisted of a larger syringe to suck the oil-based compound out of the vial, and a smaller syringe to inject four inches below their waistline into the ass cheek. Unsurprisingly, some of the guys were afraid to do the injections themselves, so in those cases, it was on me to inject it into their ass cheeks. This is where more of my favors came in down the line.

I would charge them $1,000 for PEDs that cost me $150 in Tijuana. I mean, I carried all the risk, and with that risk came charges. No one complained. After all, it's not like they couldn't afford it. Keep in mind that I was the one hustling vials of drugs from Mexico each month taped to my legs and under my balls. I was the one with the connections, the know-how, and the means with which to get these boys that much closer to a $20 million contract with the NFL. And they knew it. They just had to play by the rules and not fuck up their piss tests. We all skirted around the tests because we knew in advance when they were due to occur. We'd take the drugs all summer long but then stop one month before the season began, unless they were taking water-based Winstrol, which would be two weeks on the safe side. Our piss would be clean and clear as fresh spring water.

With my new reputation came a new name: *O-Dog.* Or *Doctor O-Dog* for the athletes scoring pharmaceutical drugs. Whether it was the athletes buying PEDs or students getting coke or Molly or E, they would spot me at clubs and restaurants all over town and buy my date and me a drink. It was a power move I didn't even have to arrange. I'd be enjoying dinner with a new date and before I knew it a bottle of Dom Pérignon would be placed on the table with the waiter saying "Courtesy of the gentlemen at the bar, sir." I'd glance over and there'd be two of my customers flashing me a grin and a thumbs-up. "They say please enjoy the champagne... *O-Dog.*" Maybe the waiter would wince and say this last part a little awkwardly, but it was always cause for a laugh with my dates.

"What are you, famous or something?" they'd gasp, eyes wide, mouth open as the waiter expertly uncorked the champagne and poured it into her glass. It was *that look* that did me in. The way these girls stared at me with unconcealed awe and curiosity . . . it filled me with an indefinable mix of feelings. Pride? Fulfillment? Ego? Whatever it was, it was something that made me feel incredibly alive. And it was my way of flipping the bird to the incessant and all-powerful concept of the American Dream.

I call it the American Nightmare: You're middle-aged, working some desk job pushing papers for higher-ups who look down on you while presiding over a company that doesn't even know your name. You're a small metric on their balance sheet, a cog in their machine, a tiny, infinitesimal piece of their whole. For you, each day is indistinguishable from the day that came before. The things you most look forward to are your bland egg-salad sandwich and your Starbucks macchiato, maybe even a smoke break here and there—those guilty pleasures from which you get your serotonin and nicotine bumps, just enough to keep you from realizing how awful your life is. Once you're done for the day, you go home and eat a microwave dinner, then zone out at the television until your eyes are dry and you're ready for sleep.

This is your every day. Monotonous routines and dull gray offices. You end each one as dispassionately as when you click the off button on your TV remote. There's no underlying hope for something more because you've become subservient to the status quo. You've played into the famous Rockefeller quote: "I don't want a nation of thinkers, I want a nation of workers." And you gave him exactly what he wanted.

When people would give me this look, the greatest satisfaction was that it simply derived from me breaking the rules of society, saying "Fuck You" to Uncle Sam, and just living happily under the banner of my own freedom. Call it ignorance; it was. Call it naïveté.

And call it what it was and has always been for me: unbridled ambition. I wanted people to come to me for anything the average joe simply did not have access to. I wanted to be the Jeff Bezos of the "other" side, the dark side: the place normal people were too afraid to traverse and now the place where I was beginning to thrive. I didn't care if I had to fly all the way to Colombia to examine the product or head north to Humboldt County to line up a hundred pounds of the best outdoor California bud money could buy. It didn't matter, because I could name whatever price I wanted with these rich USC kids, as they didn't have the balls to do what I did.

Coming from a blue-collar background that hammered home the fact that I could never get ahead like the kids born with silver spoons in their mouths, I knew one of my only options was to use my charisma and go-get-'em attitude to make seemingly anything possible for these people, and thereby for myself. I was no longer at school for an education in business or history or whatever: I was in it for an unofficial degree in networking. The only difference was that my network was the one nobody sees.

I wanted to golf eighteen holes with the congressmen and dine with the movie stars and the Hollywood elite as if I were cut from the same cloth, all with the proper etiquette and finesse so none of these people would even remotely suspect I came from a poor background. I wanted to fit right in while playing some liar's dice at the clubhouse, finishing up with a BLT and Grey Goose on the rocks and leaving you with an eight ball of cocaine, ten ecstasy pills, a Viagra, and a Xanax to help you fall asleep after the party, as I knew you were about to take a Maxim model out to the hottest club on Sunset Boulevard, where I'd call my boys Josh and Frankie to ensure that you were treated like rock-star royalty and seated in the best section next to the A-list celebrities. After all, that's why you used people like me. At least for one night, you wanted to feel like a rock star. But in reality, once you tried a taste of my shit, you wanted that feeling every night of the week.

CHAPTER 3

"Owen Michael Hanson," the loudspeaker said, and the crowd fucking roared.

It was Friday, May 13, 2005, the day I graduated from the University of Southern California and was finally free to go out into the world and carve a life for myself. What that entailed, I wasn't yet sure—nor did it matter because all I could focus on was walking down that aisle, up the metal stairs, and shaking Neil Armstrong's hand to collect my college diploma. *The first man on the moon is shaking my fucking hand right now.* Little did ol' Neil know that in a few hours I was going to have half of fraternity row in outer space with my new "moon rock MDMA" that I had purchased from an operation out of Canada.

I sprinted up those steps, clasped Neil's hand, and held that piece of paper up. I was met with five hundred faces looking out amidst the camera flashes, time slowing with the muted hum of clapping hands. Eyes on me poking out through a sea of smiles and nods, and a whole field full of hope for the great future of their children. For my future. My eyes scanned the crowd until they settled on my parents and sister. I couldn't help but smile back at them. In those moments, your joy cannot be contained. And why should it? This is one of the proudest moments of your life. *You've made it,* you think to yourself. *There's nowhere to go but up.*

I can see that scene playing out before me as if it were on the old television in the rec room, the one behind a cage of metal, like the cage I now sleep in each night. I can see all those encouraging faces, all that happiness, all that promise of things ahead. And there's me, freezeframe, smiling without an ounce of foreknowledge that the next time my name would be announced in such an authoritative tone, it would be by U.S. District Judge William Hayes at my sentencing, and the words would be "Mr. Hanson, it's hard to understand how you ended up here. By anyone's definition, you were at the top. And you were at the top for a very, very long time." He would conclude it by saying "Owen Michael Hanson, the United States Government sentences you to a 255-month sentence, twenty-one years and three months, with ten years of supervised release." The gavel would fall with an empty, hollow thud, and I would be ushered in handcuffs from the courtroom by U.S. Marshals—more like they dragged me, as my legs gave out—the last look on my father's face that of horror and sorrow and shame.

But that was a later issue. For now, I had a graduation party to attend.

After a heartfelt sendoff from USC president Steven Sample, my family and I went to El Cholo Mexican restaurant, where the USC kids went after football games. We mowed down on dozens of El Cholo tacos and enchiladas and slugged crisp margaritas. My folks treated me like I was their golden boy. I was one of the only college graduates in my family. By the looks on their faces, you'd have thought I'd gone to the fucking moon right alongside Neil.

"So, what's next?" they asked. "Got any big plans?"

The truth was I didn't really know what I wanted to do. I couldn't envision a future outside of USC, where I'd just spent the most glorious years of my life. I was now moderately wealthy, had a degree from one of the most elite colleges in the country, was at the top of my game in fitness . . . there were so many opportunities at my feet, I was like Steve Jobs with decision fatigue, which is why he always wore the same outfit, so he wouldn't have to choose a new one each morning. What Judge Hayes would later say couldn't have been truer than that present moment at El Cholo with my family. Talking with them, I realized not only had I *made* it, I was actually just getting started. *There's* more *to all this?* I asked myself. *More happiness? More success? More fun?*

I would soon find out that the unequivocal answer was: Yes.

That night, we partied as if an asteroid was on a direct collision course with Earth. In our minds there was no tomorrow; this was our last night of USC fun before going off to grad school, heading into business, or joining the NFL. I took my half pound of moon rocks—yes, they were actually named that because they looked like moon rocks—and started handing them out to students at the Beta House, our first party. They had flasks full of Jack Daniels with our names lasered on for all us graduates, as well as custom Cartier pens, one alone costing more than double my dad's mortgage. We partied for several hours until limos picked us up to take us out to the Les Deux nightclub to meet up with my teammate Matt Leinart, who was about to embark on a career with the NFL as Kurt Warner's backup. Matt was dating Paris Hilton at the time. Twenty of my frat brothers and I had two tables reserved, and we were rolling, drinking, and smoking cigars like we were the kings of Los Angeles.

Even though I was high as hell from the drugs and three sheets to the wind on the booze, I remember a long, quiet moment when all the sounds muffled and I watched my friends having the time of their lives, wondering where they would be in a year, in ten, in twenty. Would they ever be this happy again? Would they wish they had done things any different? Would I? I knew that this was one of those moments you never forget; the kind you look back on with fondness for the rest of your life. The moment that serves as a way-point, a benchmark in your memories, a place you can point to and say "Hang on, pause: you see that frame? Zoom in. That's it! This is where everything changed . . . from that night on, it was all different."

So strange, I thought, actively witnessing a memory in real time. I was in that halfway space between dreams and reality, the same one between yesterday and tomorrow, and I could see through the lens as if I'd been a clairvoyant on the periphery of human comprehension. Through all the fun and excitement and mayhem came a message of some sort: it was thick in the air; I could cut it with a sword. *Today,* it said, *is your last chance.*

My senior year in college, I had an internship, provided by the Public Policy and Development School at USC, with a recent USC graduate who worked for a prominent real estate developer. At the same time, I was studying for my real estate license under Coldwell Banker, and now I was a licensed real estate agent working for O&S Holdings, the same firm I'd interned with back at college.

O&S Holdings was owned by the founder of Kinko's, Paul Orfalea, a USC graduate, and his cousin Gary Safady, my boss. It was glamorous work: handling his laundry, arranging his extra-marital affairs, helping him hire a personal butler—as it happened, I got an old high school friend to do it—and, more importantly, handling the building of his new Hollywood Hills mansion where he'd keep his women on the side for chunks of time. I was never taken seriously—just the jock of the office, more like an ornamental plant that sat in the corner. Every now and then I would be brought out to flash my championship rings, getting called into the office or the conference room for prospective investors to leer at: "He was with the Trojans!" my boss would declare. "They had a whole season 14–0!" He would even get me to grab some of my old USC contacts, some of whom were still playing, and take us and some sorority girls all out to dinner at nice Hollywood restaurants and clubs just so he could feel "young" again.

To them, I was just the son of a construction worker who'd lucked his way into a good job through his football contacts. Sometimes on trips to pick up my boss's laundry, I'd spot a game on the TV in the dry-cleaner's, and there would be some of my old football buddies from USC scoring touchdowns for the NFL to the screams of seventy thousand people in packed stadiums. I thought of the afterparties, the clubs, the girls, the travel all over the country in private jets. The beautiful homes and brand-new cars. . . .

"Sir, are you all right?" A small Mexican lady stood at the counter of the dry-cleaner's, waiting, snapping me from my daydream and thrusting me back into reality with a confused look on my face.

"Oh, right. Sorry."

"Mr. Safady's shirts are ready."

I took the pressed Gucci shirts and custom suits off the counter, tossed them in the car, and delivered them to my boss's house. I would listen to the games on those car rides too. I could almost envision myself at one of them, not as a fan but as a player. The roar of all those fans, the bright stadium lights, the soft green turf, and the feel of a football in my gloved hands. If only I had been six inches taller. If I had run a faster forty. If I. . .

So many "ifs."

My money hadn't run dry, the job paid okay, but I wasn't flush with it either. I had stopped dealing drugs after graduation, and now everything felt . . . empty. Like I was an automaton programmed for the same tasks, day in and day out. The same things I had taken for granted back at USC, I now longed for. This world was alien and strange; there was no longer a community for me to thrive in, or a purpose to seek out. I was in a company whose founder looked at me like a glorified errand boy. There was no real possibility of advancement. It's not like one day I would have my name up there on an office door.

For more times than I was comfortable with, I found myself asking "Why?" Why this company? Why this douchebag? Why take all this shit? Why are you doing what you always said you'd never do?

While looking for an answer to all the "whys," the collapse of the real estate bubble in 2007 put me out of a job. I was the first one at the company to get axed. "Sorry, bud," my boss told me at the end of our lunch, making pen-signing motions to the waiter, who quickly came over with the check. Mr. Safady bent down over it, scribbling. He said, casually, "But you know, there are always more opportunities. And you're a bright kid." He extended his hand. "Was nice knowing you."

I walked away from that meeting as the sun fell below the horizon, setting Santa Monica Boulevard on fire in neon pink. I imagined I was still at USC. I'd just gotten done with a successful meeting with a new athlete who needed some PEDs for himself and his friends. $10,000 for the whole season I'd just earned, all in advance. I was happy, walking slowly along the boulevard and peering into all the shops and restaurants, deciding what I wanted to do for the night. I would eat at the Brazilian steakhouse, I decided, where the bartender would be impressed with my knowledge of cachaça, setting me up one cocktail after another with all the new specialties he was getting straight from Rio de Janeiro. "Try this, boss. Check out the nose on that one. You taste the Christmas spices?" I would order a flank steak, rare, slathered in chimichurri sauce, and flirt with the beautiful girl beside me who was in town on business. At the end

OWEN HANSON and ALEX CODY FOSTER · 79

of the evening, we would head back to her hotel, where the party favors in my pocket would keep us up fucking all night long until the sun climbed up over the San Bernardino Mountains, beckoning me home. Then it was a luxurious ride back to campus in a cool morning breeze, back to the frat house, and I'd slip into my soft bed to sleep until the afternoon, waking with my friends, brothers, customers, classmates. Eternity in the air and no end in sight. God, I missed that feeling. . . .

I did find myself eating at that Brazilian steakhouse, but the waiter did not give me free rounds of booze, the girl beside me did not speak, and I went home dejected and alone, waking up in the morning to a flood of gray filtering through the windows and the full weight of uncertainty of not knowing what the fuck I was meant to do in life.

At some point that morning, my dad called. "O, you see the Eagles game last night? Fuckin' A, felt bad for the poor bastards."

I didn't have the heart to tell him I'd just been fired. I just listened to him for a while talking about the game. "Uncle Tony won ten Gs on it," he said, and suddenly . . . I had it.

Back when I'd been with O&S, part of my duties as a "project engineer" was working directly for the real estate developer, showing up to meetings in California, Texas, and Louisiana with architects, city planners, engineers, and subcontractors. This was because the project manager and the project engineer represent the owner of the development company and the property owner. I oversaw documenting change orders and requests for information (RFIs), in addition to being in charge of value engineering, keeping daily meeting minutes, pulling permits, and ordering plans for the contractor with new changes. Contrary to what my boss thought of me, I actually did a whole lot of shit. And I met a whole lot of people along the way—gamblers, in particular.

I first met Andrew Parker from Parker Builders when he became the contractor on two projects I was working on for the developer. They were Foothill Crossings out of Corona and The Boardwalk in Bossier City, Louisiana, both outdoor shopping and lifestyle centers. Before our meetings, Andrew would often call his bookie to place $5,000 bets on a Thursday night NFL game. Sometimes he placed four bets at once. Twenty Gs was just a drop in the bucket for this guy who was charging the company millions of dollars per buildout. The eureka moment for me was: What if *I* was that bookie?

I had already been running bets my entire life. Gambling was in my blood. Even at twelve years old, I was a natural hustler. If there was any way I could bet on something and have a slight edge, I was there. I'd never bet unless I had that "edge," the small advantage in which my competition didn't even realize I was hustling him.

Back in junior high, I would tell my friend Joey—who had thirty pounds on me—I could beat him sprinting from one end of the soccer field to the other. He would say "No way you can beat me. You're on!" I'd wager my ice-cold Squirt on Saturday—my dad only allowed me one per week, on Saturdays—and Joey would bet a Coke from his dad's fridge today. I'd win by ten feet every time, him not knowing that those Cokes he'd drink after school each day were contributing to his baby fat and keeping him from beating me. It was a glorious cycle, and I got a Coke pretty much any time I wanted.

Later, I started betting on the handball court. I'd bring quarters I took from the change bag in my dad's pickup, telling Pops I was going to the vending machines. He'd give me a dollar, and I'd turn that dollar into five bucks by the end of PE class. I'd have my buddies tossing quarters against the handball wall: the one that landed closest to the wall took home all the quarters. Little did my friends know that I'd been practicing tossing quarters against my garage door for the last month. I knew it was all in the toss: start high and drop it in so it basically collapsed against the wall rather than bouncing off it. My friends would roll their quarters, flip, flick, and throw them. Still they couldn't figure out how I was beating them day in and day out. By the time our coach realized we were gambling, I'd already wiped out their piggy banks.

Playing basketball against my dad every night he got home from work, getting my ass whooped because he was a college basketball star, was great practice. I would utilize that practice by telling my friend John I bet I could beat him one on one. "If I win," I'd say, "I get your burrito at lunch. If you win, you can have my whole lunch tray." I'd beat him by a few points and score that burrito. I didn't want his whole tray, I wasn't a savage, but betting mine made it all too enticing for him so he wouldn't say no.

This mentality carried over to betting on the Super Bowl, on eighteen holes of golf, and even on the Presidential election. A light bulb suddenly came on, igniting the grayness of the room. Still on the phone with my dad, I came back to the conversation. "Dad. I want you to set me up in a meeting with Uncle Tony."

Some people dream of becoming a doctor or a lawyer. I wanted to be a fucking bookie.

Why the hell not? I already had extensive contacts in the construction industry. And it wasn't like I was going to become some gambling kingpin; I would be going after blue-collar guys who had a few hundred bucks to spare each week. The same guys I could sell a gram of coke to on the side, and they'd have a couple cold beers in front of the TV on the weekends watching the game.

But first I needed to speak with Uncle Tony.

I first met Uncle Tony when he was a manager at Spyder Surf back when I was a kid. He was in his forties, bald, Italian, and dressed like a surf grom half his age. He had grown up with the founders of the sports betting company in question, Macho Sports. Tony had ringside seats watching the operation grow from a fledgling garage setup to a full-blown empire over the course of a decade. Being a teacher and a bookie didn't exactly go hand in hand, however, and Tony was ready to give up the business, which meant he had thirty clients under his belt who he was willing to part with.

I met him at a diner off Sunset Boulevard. He sat in a booth at the very back. When he saw me, his eyes lit up and he stood to embrace me. "Owennnnnn, my boy," he said, laying a fat Italian kiss on my cheek. "How are things?"

"Not so good, Uncle Tony. Not gonna lie."

He nodded grimly. "I heard about the job."

I shrugged. "In this economy, it's all about survival. That's why I'm here."

He pursed his lips. We sat down and I ordered a cup of coffee. "Your pops, he's not real crazy about the idea," Tony said. "He says he doesn't want you getting into this line of work and I'm an asshole for even meeting with you."

"You know my dad, he's a blue-collar guy, worked the same job for the last thirty years. I got an education. I'm interested in putting it to use."

Tony laughed. "With sports betting?"

"No, entrepreneurship. This is just going to be one little rung on the ladder for me. All I'm asking is to meet the guys. I know sports. Not only that, but I have a huge network of USC guys who'd want to start betting. I have the construction-business guys. It's not really a big deal, it's a gray area. You know that. The servers are offshore in Peru, as are the call centers and the whole operation. And besides, this is just going to be a side gig. My buddy Sean Elliott, his dad owns a framing company that handles the structural buildouts of residential and commercial buildings. He passed my résumé on to some USC contractors out of the South Bay, and I already got a job interview set up in Torrance. I'm going to get that job, I know it."

But Tony was dubious. "Side gig?"

"Yeah, like you. This isn't your main hustle, it's just a small thing."

"I mean, I wouldn't say *that*. It gets addictive, Owen. It can become a dangerous game, and your dad has every reason to be concerned."

"I won't get addicted." I leaned in. "Listen, back at USC I was the go-to black-market concierge. Anybody and everybody knew me as the guy who could get you things. I spent the last four years making strategic bets and I never got into any sort of trouble. I know what I'm doing, Uncle Tony. I'll be smart about this. My dad's got nothing to worry about."

Tony looked at me for a long minute, then smiled and told me the story behind Macho Sports. It was founded by Leo and Bo, a pair of half Peruvian, half Norwegian brothers who grew up in Santa Monica and went to high school with Tony. They were bookies back in the '90s, big ones; they basically ran the scene in L.A. But they got so big that they had to go offshore to protect themselves. In the early 2000s, they started running their business in the legal gray area of Peru where they had some family connections. They were able to pay off the local police, so their office enjoyed immunity. These guys made over $20 million a year out of Lima just doing sports betting, and they were fucking untouchable.

"See?" I said. "It's totally above-board. I can do this, Uncle Tony. I've already got clients lined up."

Uncle Tony nodded, then slapped his hands together. "All right, kid. This is what we'll do. I'll bring you under my wing. Whatever you make, I get a percentage of. You round up some more players for us, and I'll give you ten percent for each one."

I thought back to Andrew Parker, the high-rolling gambler who'd lost a million dollars in one year. Ten percent of that would be a hundred grand. My eyes were saucers. I extended my hand. "Done. And if possible, I'd like to meet the owners face to face."

"I'll see what I can do," he said.

The next day, I got a call. It was Tony. "Pack your bags: we're going to Peru."

Apparently Tony had told the brothers about my football career back at USC. He said I'd just gotten out of college and was hungry. So they flew us both first class. Leo and Bo had us picked up at the airport in a bulletproof Range Rover. They had two security guys, one driving and one in the back, both armed with handguns and machine guns. "Holy shit," I muttered under my breath. Uncle Tony chuckled. This was all par for the course.

The security guys drove us to the office, which was right by Miraflores, the Beverly Hills of Peru. The office was three stories, all glass, and had underground parking with armed security at the gate. Against the backdrop of the ramshackle huts dotting the hillsides it looked strange and out of place, like it belonged in the fashion district of New York. We passed through a beautiful courtyard decorated with tropical trees and flowers where people sat drinking coffee. We entered a large open room resembling a call center filled with dozens of people sitting at desks speaking on phones in English.

"It's like Wall Street," I said.

Tony nodded. "One day it'll be bigger than Wall Street."

We were led to our rooms above the offices, which could have passed for luxurious suites at the Four Seasons. On the top floor were two penthouses for the brothers, where they would stay if there was a late-night football game and they needed to be boots-on-the ground managing bets and answering phones with the top players. Some professionals working late crashed on their office couches; these guys had literal fucking penthouses at their office.

After Uncle Tony and I had freshened up, we were taken by our armed chauffeurs to a high-end restaurant in Miraflores to meet the founders, who sat waiting at a small table toward the back of the joint, beaming as we approached.

"O-Dog! So nice to finally meet you!"

They stood, extending their hands. In his mid-forties, Bo was bald as a baby: cleanshaven, shaved head, bicked. He had vitiligo, patches of pure milky-white skin dotting his face and arms. But his daily workouts made him ripped like a boxer, and he was probably on some kind of testosterone therapy too. He wore all the top designer clothes: Gucci, Louis Vuitton, Prada. Leo, on the other hand, had the face of a mob boss with the build and temperament of a bulldog. He was older and thicker, and he never smiled. I could tell from the moment I shook his hand that it was pure business with him.

On the table were about a dozen different variations of the Peruvian pisco sour. We had originals, grape piscos, passionfruit piscos, Macchu piscos. Leo, I realized, was the ball-buster of the duo. He was the head of operations, the guy you wouldn't want to test your luck with. Still stone-faced, he regaled us with stories about collections he'd had to make back in the U.S. with delinquent movie producers and professional poker players: your typical old-school bookie who simply wanted to be paid in full and on time, no excuses, and no bullshit. He was boujee; within twenty-four hours he would be taking me to the spa where we'd watch NFL football, pisco sours in hand, all the while receiving massages, manicures, pedicures, and wet shaves, and eating the best ceviche I have ever tasted, as if the sea bass had been caught fresh that day—knowing Leo, it probably had, and for him personally.

Over dinner, Bo drilled me on the professional sports players I knew, and I mentioned some of my former teammates who were now dominating Sunday night football. He watched me carefully, his hand cradling his chin and his eyes glimmering like I was some kind of museum specimen. "You must come back to Peru . . . and when you do, bring one of your old teammates. We will show him the time of his life!"

He laughed. Leo simply nodded.

"I know the perfect guy," I said, and proceeded to tell them about my All-American pal Brandon Hancock. Leo couldn't have been happier. This was a guy who obsessively watched every sport. Not only was it his vocation, but it was also his passion and his way of life. He watched more sports than my pops, Big Jim, and that's saying something.

The next several days were composed of nonstop drugs and debauchery. We went to the hottest clubs and restaurants in Lima. The brothers took me to their homes, where they each had gorgeous trophy wives who looked like models, 20,000-square-foot compounds with ten nannies, private chefs, and a fleet of 24/7 security. Their homes were in a private gated community overlooking a golf course. Unable to hide my admiration, Bo put a hand around my shoulder. "The sky is the limit in this business, O-Dog. One day when you get bigger and have a nice bankroll, you can be a fifty-fifty partner like some of our best agents, and you can have all this too. Tony tells us you have great contacts. Try to provide us with some Hollywood celebrities, professional athletes, and high-powered folks. You got what it takes for this business. You got charisma, and I see you have drive. My advice? Use them."

By the time I got home, I'd not only landed the gig at a thirty percent commission, I also got the job at Del Amo Construction as a project engineer overseeing builds on schools, churches, shopping centers, and even a USC Credit Union that was going to be twenty stories tall. I could work in the office of the construction company and, all day long, book sports bets with the contractors, subcontractors, and construction workers. The blue-collar guys would lose a couple hundred bucks a week, the superintendents would lose $500 a week, and the owners of the company would lose $20k a week. The losses—and my gains—started pouring in.

Upon my return, I immediately called up Andrew Parker and gave him a proposition: I would provide him a 10 percent discount on his losses; so if he lost $100k per week, he would pay me $90k. I would always pay him within twenty-four hours after NFL weekend ended and deliver his earnings to his home in cash with never an excuse like the current bookie he was working with. I would also provide him with an additional 10 percent of "free plays" if he paid me by Tuesday; for example, 10 percent of $100k is $10k in free play, which means he would have ten grand he could gamble with that week, and if he lost it he paid nothing. If he won, he could collect the money. Why did I offer this? Because it was an insanely tempting incentive to keep him gambling, keep him losing, and keep him filling my coffers with his compounding losses. I was offering a fat kid a cake, and he could eat the whole fucking thing—and eat he would: every week, every month, my biggest whale accruing gambling debts that went directly into my pocket. To make the deal extra sweet and downright impossible to pass up, I said I would provide him with all the extracurricular activities he ever wanted, becoming his concierge at any hour, day or night. Coke? Ringside tickets? Girls? VIP treatment at the hottest clubs? My O-Dog days were back in full force, and I would make sure he had anything he wanted.

The biggest reason, however, was this: I knew this guy was a degenerate gambler and an addict in every human vice: drugs, booze, girls, gambling. Furthermore, I knew he was addicted and simply could not stop himself. My model worked better than I could have imagined. Andrew would get his $10k free play on Tuesday, and from then until Sunday he would chase that credit line I provided, usually ending with him being down far past the $10k credited; numbers like $20k to $50k in losses for the sheer fact that he could not stop, and that money went into my pocket—well, and Macho's and Uncle Tony's pockets too.

I extended this offer at his construction office over a series of blueprints, ending with "It's a win-win scenario for you, Andrew."

He nodded, smiling. "I'll give you a shot at this." He extended his hand and I shook it. "And we'll discuss the concierge service as I need things along the way."

And just like that, I went from broke and unemployed to working with one of the biggest sports-betting companies in the country, and the age-old axiom rang true:

The house always fucking wins.

A week later, I had called up all my fraternity brothers and almost every member of the USC football and volleyball teams I'd been part of. I called in every old favor owed to me from the guys who I used to shoot PEDs into their asses for, to every single friend and acquaintance and black-market concierge customer I'd retained over the years. "O-Dog! Yeah, man! I'll do anything for you. That spring break was fucking legendary!" It was a very large Rolodex, and all I asked of them was one simple thing for good ol' O-Dog:

"Do you know anybody who bets on sports?"

A lot of these guys were already gambling on sports through some bookmaker at their local sports bar, who would write bets down on pen and paper and hopefully be there the next day to pay you. But most of the time these guys were "fly by night" bookies; if they had a bad weekend, they were nowhere to be found. These were the shoddy bookies you'd find in the back rooms of strip clubs and hole-in-the-wall sports lounges where the floors reeked of piss and vomit and stale beer, and the clientele would usher you into some dark corner for a ten-dollar blowie. These guys were all too happy to leave their bookies and come to my side, blowie or not.

I started tapping the network effects of these relationships. Maybe I'd do all right and only get one or two more customers through a guy—his uncle Sal and Sal's old drinking buddy at the local watering hole, who could each pony up a couple hundred a week on bets. Or maybe I'd hit a little jackpot and get one of my fraternity brothers to tap their network of high rollers and silver-spooners, and suddenly I'd have six guys willing to blow through a grand a week. Hell, even *one* of those guys was worth more than the two previous guys put together. So I began, more and more, working the little avenues of illegal entrepreneurship I was cultivating. What benefitted my sports book? What didn't? Where was I wasting time, and how could I stop doing that shit and devote more time to higher productivity?

There were two forking paths, I soon realized. At first, Path A led me to the dingy strip clubs and sports bars with piss-streaked floors. These were a far cry from my star-studded glory days at USC, where every posh new club admitted me for free based solely on the championship rings gleaming from my fingers. These shoddy joints had '80s rock music blaring, usually Guns N' Roses, some tatted-up bikers in the back, and your regulars at the bar slurping away their meager savings on cheap beer and shots of Fireball. Just so long as they could forget their woes, their jobs, their homes—and their lives. These people were no use to me, as they couldn't afford to bet—and even if they did, I'd have to chase them across all fucking

L.A. to get my money, likely only pennies on the dollar if I was even lucky. But I wouldn't be after them; I'd be here to meet some of my old football teammates' high-school buddies, relatives, or downright degenerate acquaintances who loved to bet on sports. Didn't matter if it was baseball, football, basketball, or horse racing: they had a need, and I was there to fill it. I would go through the terms of the arrangement as they casually sipped Budweiser and ate peanuts, nodding as I spoke. If I signed them, and almost always I did, that was one or two hundred bucks I'd make a week on their losses.

Then there emerged Path B: B for Best. B for Better fucking sign this one or you're eating at McDonald's for dinner like the Path A guys. These were my high rollers, my silver-spooners. Trust-fund kids, semi-professional and soon-to-be professional athletes (and some of those too), Hollywood bluebloods. These guys loved smoking cigars, drinking a Manhattan at a chic joint, and blowing through a thick wad of hundreds betting the entire NFL Sunday. Often they didn't even really care much when they lost. It was basically nothing to them, but a whole lot to me. I would dress in a white button-down and some slacks, my championship rings on just like the old days, and saunter into these fine establishments like I owned them. Usually I'd sit down with the prospective customers for a drink to go over all the little ins and outs of why my sports book was better than the one they were currently working with. Sometimes that drink turned into two, or four, or a whole hell of a lot more, and black-market concierge Owen kicked into overdrive, supplying lines of the finest Colombian stardust and pink tabs of ecstasy that would blow their minds. I'd walk out of those places two sheets to the wind with a huge grin plastered on my face, because I'd just netted customers who were going to pay me several grand over time.

After a while, going to meet these prospective customers in person became too inconvenient. L.A. is a huge place, and I couldn't stand being stuck in gridlock for two hours just for a measly Path A customer who wasn't going to pay me much. I would still usually meet with the Path B guys, as most of them liked to hang out in Marina Del Rey and Manhattan Beach, not far from where I lived in Redondo, and were always a good time. But there was a burgeoning Path C. And this one, I discovered, was better than the previous two combined.

I went to some of the VIP clubs and lounges where I used to do business back in my USC days and started cutting deals with the managers and Hollywood promoters I knew—the guys who knew all the celebrities. "Listen," I'd say, as they came up to hug me at a VIP booth with a bottle of customary champagne on the table, "I have an opportunity for you." The curiosity sparked in their eyes. They knew me as a guy who could get you things. But if it wasn't the old thing, what was it now? "I'm a prominent agent for a sports book. We're offshore, we're big, and we are legit. We already have a long list of celebrity clientele, but I want to see that list doubled. Here's what I propose: you bring me customers, big ones, and I give you a 20 percent kickback right off the top." The wide eyes widened further, the intrigue deepening. "So if you bring me Paris Hilton and she loses ten grand in a night, that's two Gs in your pocket for so much as a simple 'Hello.' What do you think?"

Fuck, yeah! is what they thought. Every. Single. Time.

Paths A and B quickly became old hat as I started hitting C with the same fervor of the gambling addicts I kept roping into my circle. I was going to the hottest clubs in Hollywood, the best restaurants—like Mastro's, Mr. Chow's, Nobu, where you needed reservations a month in advance, but I never needed one. I was also going after my USC alumni, and when those connections dried up, I went to the current Betas and SAE fraternities. But just a few weeks into steamrolling onto my new path, I hit a major roadblock.

A guy up in Beverly Hills had lost fifty grand. That was a huge payday for me. The trouble was, he wouldn't fucking pay his tab. I'd even called his dad, who owned half of Rodeo Drive. "I'm calling in regard to your son Johnny and a delinquent tab he has with my organization." He responded saying he'd cut off his son and would no longer be paying off his gambling debts. The motherfucker would dip and dodge me. A week went by, then two. Three. Okay, $50K is no small debt. I decided to show up at his McMansion with my boy Kobra, a six-foot-six, three-hundred-pound Samoan Blood collector. But when we got there, as soon as I knocked, all the lights turned off in the house. I heard a gentle buzzing and craned my neck: in the corner of the roof, a small video camera was zooming in on me. "Kobra, let's get the fuck out of here." I hid my face with my shirt and quickly hightailed it.

When I got back to my office, I saw a message blinking on my answering machine. "Please stop stalking me. I now have you on camera and if you come to my home or my workplace ever again, I will call the police."

So there it was. The sleazy fuck. Rather than pay his losses, now not only did I have to foot the bill, but Tony and Macho were out a lot of money with very little recourse, certainly not legal anyway. The guy was no longer part of our sport betting, so not only were we out the loss, we lost out on all future money from this high roller. It was a lose-lose. And pretty soon, this started cropping up more with the big money losses I'd net through Path C. "Ohh, fuck you! What are you gonna do, call the cops on me? Ha!" Not like we didn't always get the money . . . there were enforcers we used, but those were a last resort, as they took 50 percent of whatever they collected. They would never actually hurt anyone, just use intimidation tactics, like show up to the office in a tank top and red bandana if they were Bloods, or if they were Crips it was a guy named Lurch who'd show up with two or three of his homies. They would call relatives like I did or send a bouquet of flowers to the wife with a note saying "Tell hubby it's time to pay up."

Over time, I realized that the best customer was the one in the middle path, the guy who lost $500 a week and could afford that loss. He would always pay on time, compared to the customer that lost $50k.

Once I fell into a rhythm, I was able to strike a balance with my two roles. When I finished work in the office at Del Amo Construction, I'd race to a Twilight Round of eighteen at the local golf course with one of my new customers. There was lots of money to be made on these golf courses and country clubs, and these guys liked to bet BIG.

———————————————

Business was booming, and I started collecting countries like coins in a jar.

I was traveling south of the border all the time now. Peru, because I had various meetings with the brothers, and I'd developed a relationship with a girl at their call center, Debbie. As more money started flowing in, I flew to Costa Rica with surfer friends from the South Bay who wanted to catch some good waves. Eventually on one of these trips I met a Colombian girl at the club who invited me back to her hometown of Medellín, birthplace of the infamous Pablo Escobar. She and I sipped dark coffee on her patio overlooking the city to the tune of incessant car horns and kids down on the dirt street below kicking a soccer ball. "My father and uncles worked with Escobar," she said reverently, gazing out at the sun fading fast below the skyline.

"What happened?"

She took a sip. "They were all killed."

That night, we visited Pablo's grave. Bouquets of flowers were strewn about the black marble gravestone, old and new, as well as little scraps of paper with messages and prayers inscribed on them. We gave him the old Colombian stardust salute, pouring a line of coke over his grave before doing a few lines ourselves. Ironically, it was here—at Pablo Escobar's grave—that I had the epiphany that would change the course of my life.

These countries I was visiting—Mexico, Peru, Ecuador, Costa Rica, Colombia—they all had an undying narco legend. Sure, in America we had the Five Families in New York, George Jung in California, as well as Frank Lucas in Harlem. We had our own drug barons and legends. But those guys were nabbed, killed, or else they operated in quiet obscurity. But in these third-world countries, narcos were folk heroes. They were more than legends. They had created entire empires that would be remembered for generations. I wondered how they had built these empires so effectively. I'd just been a kid selling coke on the USC campus, but what if there was more I could be doing with my skills?

I was making great money between the bookmaking and the construction business, but the latter was going to dry up soon, as I was nearly done with the last two projects in my contract with Del Amo: the USC Credit Union and an elementary school off Mulholland Drive. I was knocking the punch lists and closing subcontractors' RFIs and final billing, so the writing was on the wall. Luckily, I had acquired a lot of customers in my "cash" business, and not just the hammer-swinging construction workers who were good for a couple hundred bucks a week.

Also, I was now taking bets from members of the cartel.

During my travels, I started dating girls who all seemed to have one thing in common: they liked the "bad boy" archetype above all else. Maybe this was due to their living in third-world countries, where they struggled to survive, and cartel members were the richest people in their entire continent. They fell for guys their uncles and fathers worked for, narcos like Escobar, Don Neto, El Señor de Los Cielos, and the Arellano-Félix brothers. I started heavily researching these third-world folk heroes. What made them tick? How were they so successful at what they did? And what brought them down?

In the back of my mind, I knew an idea was culminating. Back in college, I was great at selling drugs, and I never once got caught for it. But that was because I was simply trying to make ends meet and keep up with the Joneses, pay for some steak dinners at the Pacific Dining Cart in downtown L.A., drink the same Johnnie Walker Blue Label as my friends, and date some sorority girls. I'll admit it was completely to meet my superficial needs, but now was different. I wasn't some green college kid anymore, trying to skate by and make ends meet on a few grand I made here and there. I wasn't just trying to keep up with the Joneses; I was avidly pursuing entrepreneurial endeavors that filled me with passion. My clientele now included CEOs of Fortune 500 companies, professional athletes, Hollywood elites, and blue bloods. Where before I had been known as the college black-market concierge who could get you whatever you wanted, now the same principles applied but on a grander and more influential scale. These people respected me, trusted me.

What if I created my own operation?

At the same time, I was taking bets from drug runners called "Narco Juniors," who represented the new era of drug trafficking. These guys were relatives of head lieutenants and bosses in the largest and most dangerous drug cartels of Mexico . . . these same guys would routinely land a mattress in a six-by-eight cell for twenty years, but for the moment, they were my customers. The best part about them was that they were never short on cash, which was dropped by them just like the quarters I used to toss against the handball court to hustle my friends out of a few bucks. It was a drop in the bucket for them.

When the Narco Juniors would lose, they would pay me from their drug proceeds all in cash or wire it to one of our offshore Costa Rican accounts. One of these Juniors, Felix, went on a winning streak. He made $200k after an NFL weekend. I didn't know it at the time, but his uncle was one of the most powerful lieutenants for the most dangerous cartel in the world, and he had been using his nephew's betting account. Come Monday morning, I got $200k in cash in a suitcase and had it hand-delivered to his people in Corona. My punctuality with this business dealing would put me on the radar of his uncle.

Just like my numbered days with Del Amo Construction, I could see the writing on the wall with Macho Sports. I wasn't somebody who could sit and do the same thing for the rest of my life—and certainly not when I thought I could do it better. Now I had enough money to go to Costa Rica, the mecca of sports betting, and open my own operation. I had made a name for myself in the industry and knew all the top bookmakers. Some of my customers were losing seven figures on the sports book I was working for. That included the narcos.

Why was I paying these brothers 70 percent on my customer losses? I ran the numbers: if I booked the action myself and hired a staff to run my site, call center, and move my odds based on Las Vegas sports books betting lines, my profits would come close to 90 percent. My whole life up to this point had been a gamble. What did I have to lose?

My reputation in the business was high partly because I was so good at recovering losses. I was done getting hung up on or, worse, calling lines that had become disconnected. I figured why not hire a private investigator to track them down? I met Danno Portley-Hanks one day at a coffee shop off the 405 freeway. His name was passed down to me from another Macho Sports colleague, and supposedly this guy Danno was an "agent to the stars."

True to his name, Danno was portly. He was dressed in a triple XL polo and oversized slacks, his protruding belly pushing the table toward me as he sat. His white hair was slicked back, and he resembled a beat cop from the old film noir movies. He said he was Tom Cruise's own private investigator and had even worked with the FBI. He had information that agencies like the FBI, CIA, and DEA had access to. According to him, his database was "out of this world."

"How hard would it be for you to find them?" I asked.

"Do you have their full name?"

"Yes."

"Then I can find anything you want. Their home address, family members' addresses, phone numbers. Anything."

So I started working these guys who wouldn't pay, making them sweat. I would call them, saying "Listen, I know your mom lives at 1224 Arena Drive. I would hate to go down there and recover the debt from her. Why don't you just pay up?" Some of these scumbags didn't care about their families, but 85 percent of them did, and they paid.

The other factor that helped bolster my career was that I was the best at netting high-roller customers due to my USC connections. I started landing clients from Vegas who lived in $20 million homes. I was giving casino hosts kickbacks just like I did with the managers at VIP clubs and restaurants in L.A., and pretty soon my Rolodex was bursting with the numbers of the top 1 percent.

Macho Sports had an overseas VIP customer, Chang, flying into Vegas with $10 million he wanted to bet. The brothers wanted me to join him so he had the black-market concierge experience. I and five other VIP agents were picked up by this customer in a private G6 jet at LAX. The Macho brothers were playing backgammon with Chang as I pounded vodka sodas and tried to get my date into the bathroom so I could join the Mile High Club.

"They're gonna know," she said, giggling.

"So what!"

"What if they kick us off the plane?"

"You mean DB Cooper style, with parachutes?"

She pinched me. "Lead the way, you goof."

Suffice it to say, I made it into the aforementioned club, which could only portend that the ensuing weekend was going to be a blast.

We landed in Vegas an hour later with a fleet of Town Cars and Escalades awaiting us. They took us to the newly constructed Aria Casino, which cost a whopping $9.2 billion. Upon arrival at my penthouse overlooking the Las Vegas Strip, I was met by my own personal butler. He greeted me at the door with a bucket of ice-cold Cristal champagne. "Sir, your room," he said, ushering me inside to one of the most extravagant penthouse suites I'd ever seen. Through the floor-to-ceiling windows, the lights of Vegas glittered like tiny diamonds and bits of gold, all its luster and depravity ripe for the taking.

Bo and Leo had made sure I brought some of my NFL contacts to schmooze the client amidst all the wining and dining, snorting and fucking that was sure to ensue. I'd invited Derek Loville, Reggie Bush, and Jeremy Shockey. I had also invited a harem of the hottest girls I knew back in Hollywood. All of them had their flights booked and comped hotels courtesy of Macho Sports.

We got tables at Haze Nightclub and bungalows at Rehab Pool Party, which was Spring Break 24/7 with DJ Tiësto performing. We ate $500-an-ounce Beluga caviar and washed it down with Cristal and Dom Pérignon. The VIP was losing hundreds of thousands at the baccarat tables. Within forty-eight hours, he had lost nearly six million dollars.

I was caught up in the glitz and glamor of it all, but in the back of my mind there was a nagging feeling of doubt. Surely this couldn't last forever. Would I want it to? What was my end goal, and why was I here?

Chang's six-million-dollar loss turned to ten, and he took his private jet back home to South America with the brothers, leaving us young hooligans languishing by the pool on our fourth straight day of non-stop booze and coke. I was in and out of consciousness, high and drunk and drifting through the ether of multiple distorted realities—when I saw her.

Across the pool was a small group comprised of the Black Eyed Peas' manager and some of the bandmates, as well as several beautiful women. I'd just finished snorting the last of my stardust, my head instinctively whipping upward as I inhaled it, the sky cloudless and immense past the expanse of skyscrapers along the periphery of my vision. Planes soaring overhead as if in slow motion. A feeling of sudden, warm euphoria spreading over me like I'd just slipped into a warm bath. I felt I was up there in that endless sky, with the planes. When I finally brought my head down, my eyes fell on the group across the pool, settling on a gorgeous Latina woman. She met my eyes and smiled. The feeling of euphoria from that smile alone superseded every ounce of blow I'd ever snorted.

I spoke in Spanish: "Hello, my name is Owen. What's your name?"

She giggled, and several of her friends looked at me like, *Who is this Güero? Can't he see we're busy?*

I was not prepared for the outpouring of perfect Spanish which came out of her mouth in hyper speed. She didn't speak a drop of English. I had to call my friend Gabby over to help translate. Within a few minutes I had all the information I needed: her name was Desiree Carillo, she was single, and she lived back in Beverly Hills. And she would love to go out to dinner at Nobu with me.

That was it. Case closed. This was the perfect weekend, and I had just concluded it by meeting my future wife.

I had customers all over the country who I would have cash delivered to, picked up from, and wired. Felix called me one day. "Hey, Owen, my uncle is wondering if he can pay you a ten percent service fee for any time he needs cash to pay some of his delivery guys in California, or maybe some of his workers in North Carolina and Florida." These were places I already had sports book runners moving cash, so it was an easy yes.

At this point I'd been to Peru dozens of times, and the Macho Sports brothers greatly respected me, as I was further helping to build their sports book empire. One day, over a lavish braised lamb shank dinner at a restaurant overlooking the sparkling city of Lima, I propositioned them: "What if I started my own operation?"

They seemed confused. Neither of them spoke.

"I'd use your guys' software, VoIP phones, and infrastructure," I said. "It's already there and it works perfectly. I'll have my own site, BetODog. I'll pay a set monthly fee. And when I acquire customers who are too big for me, we'll split the commissions fifty-fifty."

Bo frowned deeply and waved the idea away with the Peruvian wind. "No, no. Owen, that would be taking away from our business. It would make no sense for us. I understand your ambition, but you need to be a teammate who grows with the company, not branch off independently. This is a family business, and you are part of the family now."

Leo agreed. But I was persistent. *"Exactly.* I'm not suggesting I steal your proprietary infrastructure; I'm saying we duplicate it to make more money."

This got their attention. I continued. "We can license your software and your 800 numbers to the guys who want to be their own bookmakers; the guys who we're not even currently working with. License your bookmaking infrastructure to them for a set rate based on how many customers they have and how much money they are bringing in. For example, $50 a week per customer for unlimited internet bets and phone calls into the call center. This would create an entire side operation of cash flow for the company that didn't exist before, and I would personally manage it from my own office in Costa Rica but split my largest commissions with you guys fifty-fifty. Once the operation is scaled properly, it could bring in hundreds of thousands a month in extra revenue for the company."

It was the modern-day equivalent of using a successful app, like Uber. Macho Sports was the Uber of the sports-betting world, but they were the only ones using the app. What if they allowed other hungry bookies to use it in return for a commission? It was a win-win for everyone involved. The brothers sat in stunned silence a few moments. Then they gave a unanimous "Yes."

I already knew bookies all over the U.S. who were working with different software, shitty dial-up internet, bad phone calls, and poor Las Vegas line services that didn't move fast enough. What I offered to them was the crème de la crème of bookmaking services. Within three months, I'd signed up twenty clients, each with over a hundred customers. At two thousand customers, that was nearly half a million dollars I was bringing in already in just three months; all the brothers had to do was add more bandwidth to their already-existing servers. All they were in charge of was billing the bookies, and the bookies—unlike fickle customers you had to chase down—would *always* pay their dues, because if not, their software and therefore entire operations would be shut down.

This was why I had self-employed bookies all over the country picking up and delivering cash for me. Once I started doing it for Felix's uncle, I was making 10 percent off $50,000, $100,000, even $200,000 transactions. This might be $50k to two drivers running a hundred kilos of cocaine across the San Ysidro border to California, or I'd be dropping off $50k at a stash house in San Bernardino to guys just sitting there with guns guarding a few hundred kilos. It was the easiest money I ever made.

Felix called again. "Owen, my uncle has one million dollars in cash stored at a safe house over in Brownsville, Texas."

"What do you need me to do?"

"We would get it ourselves, but the issue is many of the rival cartels are in this area robbing everybody blind, and law enforcement has been seizing a lot of my uncle's money. People of our color are all suspicious, but you're a white boy. If you dress in a dapper suit, everyone's just going to think you're another Texas oil man. The problem is we would need the cash flown out of there, probably private."

Without hesitation, I said "I got you. I'll fly into the Brownsville Airport, a private airport right there across from Tamaulipas, Mexico. Have someone meet me with the cash in the airport parking lot and I'll fly it out and get it to your uncle within twenty-four hours."

As soon as I got off the phone, I called my buddy Levi from college, whose friend Chip was a pilot and owned a Beechcraft plane. Chip told me he charged $3,000 an hour for flights, but since we had a mutual friend he'd cut that to two grand. The route was eight hours roundtrip. "Is it just a quick pick-up?" he asked.

"Yes. I sold a catamaran and the buyer is paying me in cash."

"No problem. But listen, I have one rule on my plane: No weapons."

The idea of traveling into rival cartel territory to pick up a million bucks without any weapons to protect myself was a little disconcerting, so I called one of the original gangsters from the Avalon Crips, Tank, saying I needed a favor. I needed him to get one of his UFC friends to join him on this flight as security. "I'll pay you each two grand."

Tank seemed confused. Four grand just for a simple flight? There had to be something more to it. "What is this, O? You need us to, you know . . . fuck somebody up?"

"No, nothing like that. You two can just sit in the plane. I'll go and pick up the suitcase in the parking lot."

Tank got his UFC friend Diego to join us. We dressed in suits and met at Torrance Airport the next morning. As we walked along the tarmac toward the plane, I took a five-dollar bill from my wallet and a pocket notebook and jotted down the serial number of the bill. Then I called Felix. "Listen," I told him. "When I meet your guy, I'm going to give him a five-dollar bill. This bill's serial number is the receipt of our transaction and will signify that I'm the guy who's supposed to pick up the suitcase. Do you have a pen?" I waited as he got a pen and paper, then read him the serial number. I also snapped a picture of it on my phone. "All right, give that to your uncle to give to your delivery guy, who I'll confirm it with when he hands it off. This will mean the package has been retrieved and it's on its way in the right hands."

The Beechcraft was a bit rugged, a mid-'90s model, but it would get the job done. Chip didn't ask any questions; neither did Tank or Diego. We just hopped in the plane, put on some noise-cancelling headphones, and were underway. It was a perfect cloudless afternoon. The fifteen hundred miles passed with no issue; and when we landed at the Brownsville Airport, I sent the uncle, "El Jefe," an encrypted message on the Phantom Secure phone his nephew had given me.

I'm here.

El Jefe wrote back immediately. *He'll be there in five minutes.*

I told the guys to wait in the plane and headed to the parking lot. The next thing I knew, a beat-up old gardening truck pulled into the lot toward the back. We locked eyes, and I strode over. He grabbed a heavy duffel bag, got out of the truck, and said "Do you have the receipt?"

The gardener was dressed in stained overalls, dirt caked under his fingernails. He wiped sweat from his forehead with a handkerchief.

"Yeah." I handed him the five-dollar bill. He spent a few moments going over the serial number, matching it with his own from a torn piece of invoice. Then he nodded and handed me the duffel bag.

"This is for the boss, El Jefe."

"Let him know his money will be safe in California in four hours."

Walking back to the plane, my adrenaline was on fucking fire. My eyes darted around, at the entrances and exits, the cars, the people walking past. At any second, any one of them could unleash a hail of gunfire and I would be dead. A million dollars was in this bag. How many people would kill for a million bucks?

On the plane, Tank took one look at the bag and said, "What the fuck?"

"He paid in full," I said. "We're good to go."

I hadn't told anyone the real reason of the journey. Tank would soon find out, but I didn't want to implicate them. As soon as the plane hit the air, I breathed a massive sigh of relief, then I felt completely depleted, a hangover from the adrenaline fading away. I wondered how people did this day in and day out. Did they live for that rush? I thought of Barry Seal, the infamous American pilot who ran drugs for the Medellín cartel while working as an informant to the DEA. At his peak, Seal was making half a million dollars per flight and had a fleet of over a dozen aircraft. Did he feel this same rush?

We landed back in Torrance. I took out a stack of twenty grand from the duffel bag, paying Chip and the boys. Within thirty minutes, I delivered the money, minus my hundred grand, to one of El Jefe's safehouses. I texted him, my hands shaking. "It's done and with your guys."

That night, I slept like a fucking baby.

I was in Vegas with the brothers during the Super Bowl when I got a bet from Paris Hilton.

It came through my buddy Doug Reinhardt, a minor league baseball player who was featured on the hit reality TV show *The Hills*. We were at our own private table in Aria with a bunch of Macho Sports's top agents when I got the call from Doug. "Hey, O, Paris wants to bet on the game."

It took me by surprise. "No shit?"

"No shit," he said.

Around me, the fellas were slugging champagne like there was no tomorrow, snorting lines of coke off the table, and downing shots of Clase Azul Ultra Tequila in between slobbery bites of herb-butter snow crab and sixty-day dry-aged Tomahawk steak. Our table was the personification of gluttony, lust, and excess: gorgeous women and coked-up guys, mounds of food, all different variations of drugs and alcohol. The Super Bowl was like Christmas in the betting community, and Macho Sports was fucking Santa Claus.

"How much?" I asked, leaning into the phone to hear through the din.

"Ten grand."

I cupped the receiver and looked up at the guys. "Hey, can we take this bet that's coming in? It's ten Gs from Paris Hilton."

You could have heard a mouse fart. Suddenly everybody went silent and wide-eyed. "You're fucking with us," one of the guys said, butter dribbling down the stubble on his chin.

"No, sir. My buddy dates her. And Paris wants to bet ten grand."

There are certain events in life that grant you what the Goodfellas call *respect*. This could be through acts of service in the community, like unloading a whole cube truck of fresh turkeys on Thanksgiving to the poor families in the neighborhood or walking an old dame home holding her groceries in one arm while escorting her with the other. It could be an act of omertà, the Mafia code of silence and refusal to give up evidence linking your guys. It could also be an act of psychotic violence that helps your buddies out of a bind. In any case, when you earned their respect, you earned their adoration, their allegiance, and their support. When I looked around that table then, a glass of chilled Clase Azul Reposado in one hand, and Paris Hilton's boyfriend on the phone in the other, I knew that I had earned their respect. Here I was a twenty-something kid fresh out of college and I was already earning more than most of the top guys at Macho Sports. I was bringing in celebrity clientele and famous sports players, and engineering new entrepreneurial pursuits that were now earning the brothers millions of dollars in extra income per year. And now . . . I was taking bets from Paris Hilton.

"Well, yeah!" Leo said, like it was a no-brainer. And everyone seemed to snap out of their reverie and come back to the present moment. I firmed up details with Doug, then got off the phone. Sure enough, Paris ended up losing that bet, which made us some good money. But that wasn't the true win for me in the exchange. I couldn't help but notice that the brothers and the top agents didn't look at me like some junior with stars in his eyes, like I was viewed back at the real estate offices of King Asshole, who made me fetch his dry cleaning and iced Starbucks Macchiatos with extra whipped cream. These guys looked at me as if I was a burgeoning force to contend with, maybe even their prodigy. And I admit this felt good, and it probably got to my head, which is why no sooner had I collected that money from Paris Hilton's personal assistant than I was on a plane to Costa Rica to set up a new form of sports betting: live online casinos.

At a private dinner, I'd run the idea by the brothers that same weekend in Vegas. They shook their heads. "No, O-Dog, we need to stick to the sports. That online casino business is rigged. And besides, we don't want to make our customers upset."

"But it'll only cost us an extra couple bucks a month," I protested. "All these other bookies are doing it and they're raking in hundreds of thousands. They're live dealers! Can you imagine how big this will become? We're still at the beginning!"

This was in 2009. The era of live casinos hadn't yet begun. We could be the guys with first-mover advantage, the Microsoft and Amazon of the dot-com bubble, which left nearly 97 percent of online businesses bankrupt after it burst. The few companies that survived went on to become the best blue-chip stocks in any portfolio with the largest market caps in history at the fucking top of the monopoly. I wanted Macho Sports to be that in the betting world, not just sports betting, but *all* betting.

But the brothers would not relent. They were too old-school. I felt like Sollozzo in *The Godfather* begging Don Corleone to see the benefits of selling heroin. It was going to be on the streets anyway, whether it was Corleone backing it or some other head of the Five Families. But the Don was old-school, he didn't want that shit out there corrupting and killing the youth. For that he would pay the price: Sollozzo's hitmen shot him several times and he nearly died. Of course, I wasn't going to have the brothers shot up Mafia-style and usurp their company, but it did teach me a vital lesson in black-market business: sometimes the Boss isn't always right, or at least he isn't willing to adapt.

But I was young, brash, and hungry. After that conversation, I immediately flew down to Costa Rica, the Mecca of the betting world, where all the offshore online casinos were getting set up. I didn't even inform my surfer buddy who had a house on the beach. I showed up unannounced and offered to wine and dine him all week long if he let me crash on the couch and start networking like a madman. He loved it.

I started meeting with the heads of several burgeoning online casinos and some of the biggest bookies, under the pretense of paying rent to their call centers and $10k a month for their software. I'd create my own domains and be provided a 1-800 number—the same model I'd built for Macho Sports with all the bookies and customers under their umbrella, only this time I was the bookie, not the infrastructure provider.

My buddy's house was in Jaco Beach on the Pacific side, where pretty much every bar owner was an expatriate from the States now doing bookmaking out of his establishment. I spoke with them too. Then I went to casino offices in San Jose, where I was shown their software. I started a company called Rockstar Bets using this software. I agreed to pay a $10k fee for the initial month to test out the software and see how my customers liked the casino. But still the operation felt too slow and small. I needed my BetODog.com domain. This was what all my own customers and bookies were used to; it's what had respect in the business. And I needed my matching 1-800-BET-ODOG number. Without these, I essentially had to restart the entire betting operation that I'd worked so hard to build.

There was a grave impediment to my networking, and ironically that was Macho Sports. They had all the contacts, all the 1-800 numbers of bookies I'd set up with their own portals through Macho, the same operation that had the brothers earning millions a year and was entirely my idea. But even though I'd secured those deals, they weren't *my* customers. They belonged to Macho and worked exclusively through Macho's servers. I couldn't just go behind the brothers' backs and reach out to these customers, asking if they would like to join my online casino. I had earned the brothers' respect, and I needed to keep it.

My next trip to Peru, we sat down to discuss business, and I presented my predicament to them. "I have all the pieces in place for my own casino operation, but I'm lacking the main component: the players. I know for a fact that all these guys want a casino on their sites, and if you guys aren't going to provide that service, with respect . . . I think it's only fair that you release to me my domain name and 1-800 number so I can."

The brothers were upset. Leo paced his vast office, pinching his chin with a slight scowl on his face. *Fuck me*, I thought. *Now I've done it. I've offended my bosses. They probably think I'm going to try to become their competitor!*

Leo took a deep breath, and the scowl slid off his face. "You have earned us some good money," he said. Bo nodded in agreement. They looked at each other, a silent message passing between them. Then Leo turned back to me. "And we appreciate you coming to us and asking. You have our blessing, O-Dog. We'll release those to you."

This is how BetODog.com was born.

Within weeks I was in San Jose, Costa Rica, setting up my office on the thirty-second floor of a high-rise building overlooking the city and the rainforest beyond.

Mark was the guy who was renting the space. He let me move all my servers there and open my call center. The previous outfit running my online casino was charging me up the ass; meanwhile, I was getting complaints from hundreds of customers saying their calls were never answered, the site would routinely go offline as the servers cut out, and it was an all-around shitshow. With Mark—a recent college graduate and tech wizard who was making his bones in the offshore gambling industry—that would not happen.

As usual, this was a cash business. When Mark flew to the States every couple of months, I would take him out to the best restaurants—Madeo Ristorante in Beverly Hills and Mr. Chow—wine and dine him, then take him out to my Range Rover and hand him a duffel bag with fifty grand. It was a drop in the bucket. Between my sports book and my online casino business, I was raking in over a hundred grand a month gross. But this venture was not without risk. In the back of my mind, I constantly worried some hotshot lucky asshole betting half a million bucks was going to net a winning streak, and, since that was beyond my bankroll, it would fuck me. Aside from the sports book, I was slowly phasing out of Macho Sports, and I realized that if such a thing were to happen, I'd be up shit creek without a paddle or a pot to piss in. One solid streak could ruin me. On one hand, I felt I'd finally made my mark and was on to big things. But on the other, I realized it was a house of cards ready to fall at the gentlest breath.

I split my time between L.A., Vegas, and Costa Rica. In L.A. and Vegas, I wined and dined my clientele and sought out hosts to VIPs at the best restaurants, nightclubs, and casinos to hook their customers up with my sports book and online casino. I ran my business like a Fortune 500 company. I baked incentives into the package. If you paid up on Monday, I'd take 10 percent off your losses. If you paid by Tuesday, 5 percent. And if you paid on either day, I'd give you 20 percent in free plays. I did this because if I was paid no later than Tuesday, that gave me leeway to pay the winning customers by Wednesday or Thursday.

My schedule had never been so packed. Monday through Friday I was entertaining potential new clients, agents, and customers. We'd play golf at the country club, eat at the finest restaurants, party at the best nightclubs. There was not a second in my day that wasn't vouched for. I was up at dawn, doing cardio with my trainer from 6 to 7 a.m. By 9 a.m. I was at the country club with clients, and come noon I was five cocktails deep with a couple Vicodin and bumps of coke thrown into the mix. Then it was on to a restaurant for another batch of clients, and after that I'd get on the phone with Kenny, my manager of operations, and run all the numbers. Any hiccups with runners collecting payments? If so, why, and how could we get them to get our money? Is the software running okay? How much did we make this quarter, and how many new high-profile VIPs do we need to double that figure by next quarter?

March Madness was coming up, which meant I'd bring in my own VIP customers to Vegas in true Macho Sports fashion—hosting the best party of their lives while persuading them to toss money into my online casino once they were bored of losing at the Bellagio or Caesar's Palace. Or I'd piggyback on my famous contacts like three-time Super Bowl champion Loville, who introduced me to Chuck Liddell, Mike Tyson, and Tito Ortiz. As I had learned with Macho Sports, all these VIP guys had "hosts." I knew the brothers played host to several VIPs who'd fly in private jets to Vegas with $5 million and just lose the whole fucking pot. These guys would be given 20 percent back on their losses by the casino host, so, once they obliterated that sum, they'd get another million back to lose. It was brilliant. They were incentivized to fill the casino's coffers. I did the same thing with my VIP clients, who introduced me to *their* VIP clients, and so on. It was a constant game of networking, and being the black-market concierge that I was, I signed on customers to my sports book and online casino left and right. But again, there was that nagging suspicion that the axe was about to fall. All it would take is one of my VIP guys, roaring drunk and with a nose full of powder, to go all in on a couple million during the Super Bowl and I'd be fucked. It was all well and good and my life was a nonstop party, but I needed more cash flow. How would I get it?

During the March Madness college basketball tournament in 2010, I got my answer.

It came from the ring of an encrypted phone while I was sitting alone at the bar of the Bellagio eating Yellowfin tacos and drinking a glass of chilled tequila. It was a Phantom Secure phone that El Jefe's nephew had given me before I did the Texas money run. He told me to always have it on hand, just in case, and I did. But I had never heard it ring.

My mouth stuffed, I quickly washed down the food with tequila and took out the phone, glancing around. Everyone was drunk, high, gambling. They didn't notice the phone, which looked like any ordinary Blackberry. My heart raced. Who was calling, and why? Slowly, hand shaking, I brought it to my ear.

"Hello?"

"Owen."

Hispanic voice, smooth, self-assured. Powerful. El Jefe.

"Yes, speaking."

"What is your background?"

I told him. Football, USC, and . . . again looking around, just to be sure . . . dealing drugs back at school, black-market concierge, real estate, now my own sports book and online gambling.

He asked "Have you ever been arrested for any of these activities?"

"No, sir. I have a clean record."

Silence followed. Had I said something wrong? There was an eternity in that silence. A vacuum. Here was a guy who held the power of life and death. Then he asked "Do you have any contacts in Australia?"

I thought for a moment. "Yes, I've got an aunt over there."

"How would you like to clean some money and move some product of mine over there, if we would give you a place?"

Now it was my turn to fall silent, the enormity of his question suddenly weighing over me. One of the most powerful lieutenants in the cartel was asking me to be a narco for him. Fucking cheesy, I know, but that scene from *The Godfather* came to mind: "I'll make him an offer he can't refuse." Of course, El Jefe wouldn't have me whacked if I said no. But strangely, even though I'd never even met the guy, I didn't want to disappoint him. That old feeling I'd garnered with the Macho brothers, the VIP clients, and the top agents came rearing its egoic head—*respect*. I had earned El Jefe's respect with that Texas job. I remember the surprise in his nephew's voice when I told him the money was already in their safe house. "Already?" he'd asked, like I'd just yanked a rabbit out of a hat. Being the cartel, I figured they were used to on-time payments and jobs getting done quickly. It wasn't like my business, where you had to chase around some trust-fund punk for weeks on end, maybe dropping a threatening card in the mail to the wife. No. If you owed the cartel, you *paid* the cartel. So why was he tapping *me*?

I was in one of those moments again, I knew. Like the one I'd had the night I graduated from USC; I was partying, but everyone dancing suddenly became languid and slow. I looked around the room at the freeze-frame of my future, little text bubbles popping over the heads of graduates destined for bigger things; one bubble read "Doctor," one read "Lawyer," one read "Broker." Above my head there was nothing. No text. No destiny driving me further. I'd gotten into that school for volleyball, then was kicked off the team. I made it on the football team with zero experience, then spent the next two seasons warming the bench. I had a degree I didn't know how to use. All I was ever good at was doing what El Jefe was offering me right now.

I responded "Let me do some homework and get back to you." I paused. "But I'm sure I can get it done."

El Jefe thanked me and hung up. My moment was still right there, I was in it. The sounds of the casino softly faded to the background, all the bright lights and the people obscured right along with them. I was in my new moment of destiny, of fate, where I could decide how my life would turn out. Would I always be a bookie with a limited bankroll just waiting for the axe to fall? Or could I put my black-market concierge skills to work for the richest and most powerful crime syndicate on earth?

I downed my drink. I was going to work for the cartel.

CHAPTER 4

Homework.

I did a lot of that in school. Always cramming it between practice, workouts, rush week, parties, sex, and drugs. Now, my homework consisted of finding out how to smuggle thousands of kilos of cocaine into the most notoriously difficult country in the world to get drugs into. It was the Fort Knox of the cocaine world, only the gold was on the outside, trying to get in.

It took no time at all for me to find out why El Jefe wanted to sell his product there. Because it was Cocaine Fort Knox, the street price was four times that of New York or Los Angeles. If he could find a way to get into Australia's market, he would dominate it, which means his already obscene profits would soar, and eventually he would be one of the biggest drug kingpins in the world.

Networking again became my mantra, digging back in my mental Rolodex to find out who might possibly be able to help me with this. What came to mind was another friend from USC, a baseball player whose brother had been in the weed business in San Diego a while back. Over lunch one day, I asked my friend: "Do you think your brother knows anybody who can move large amounts of cocaine?"

"How much we talking here?"

"Lots."

He thought for a moment, then an "Aha!" look came over his face. "You know what? Funny you ask: my brother used to work with this guy he called Uncle Louie back in the day. Italian guy. Used to be the biggest weed dealer in San Diego. Anyway, as luck would have it, he's visiting my bro next week. Maybe you can head down there and you guys can chop it up."

"You'd set that up for me?"

"Of course, O-Dog."

The respect. So many people from all walks of life still felt they owed me favors. People really were the most valuable currency.

A week later, I was in San Diego knocking on the door of my buddy's brother. He let me in with a big handshake, pulling my hand in to check out the championship ring on my finger. He led me into the living room, where a mid-sixties Italian guy was sitting on the couch. He got up to greet me.

"Uncle Louie, meet Owen."

The brother got us some cold drinks, and I sat there shooting the shit with Louie for a while. He told me all about his heyday back in the 1980s, when he'd moved a lot of coke for the Lucchese family. He sold me the whole black-market American dream, my eyes wide with awe and envy as he recounted with great gusto the massive beachfront home he owned and all the accoutrements of a king. He was a living, breathing, un-incarcerated George Jung.

"I'm working with some . . . uh, *contacts*," I said, "south of the border. Since I know how to move things around pretty good, they tapped me to see if I could get their product into Australia."

"Australia!" he said. "Christ Almighty, that's the promised land. You're crazy, man. You'll never get no coke into Australia."

I nodded. "I know it'll be difficult, but. . ."

Uncle Louie waved this away. "Not impossible. I get it."

He studied me a moment, sizing me up. Then he shrugged. "Listen, I got a group o' guys outta Amsterdam that I can reach out to, but I can only reach out to 'em once I'm back in Italy 'cuz they only meet in person. I'm here visiting family. I'll be back in Italy in a month. I'll talk to my guys and get back to you."

A month later, I met him at Roma Fiumicino. He had a tiny red Fiat I could hardly fit in, and all I could do was sit in abject terror as he drove the thing like a fucking maniac, reeling out onto the main highway like a bat out of hell, cutting people off, changing lanes without using the blinker. I quickly noticed that the crosswalk signs didn't depict people slowly walking, they were *running*. With people like Uncle Louie on the road, I understood why.

He talked a mile a minute, classic Italian. It was all food and wine and women. "You've never been to Italy?" he asked, frowning as he nearly barreled into a group of Chinese tourists, who flailed their arms as they dove out of the way to avoid being hit. *"Andare! Andare!"* he hollered out the window at them as he passed. He quickly rolled the window back up and proceeded to smoke his fifteenth cigarette. I cracked mine open, feeling sick.

"Nah, in L.A. we have all the food, wine, and women a guy could want."

"No, no!" he said, waving his hands. "You kid yourself, Owen. You lack the one basic thing every man needs."

"What's that?"

"Italian women!" he laughed uproariously. Then his face soured. "Though you will never know a more complicated breed of woman."

He told me about his homes, his family, his wife. Uncle Louie owned two properties in the Tuscan countryside. He lived in his family home in Naples, and he also had a winery in Tuscany with a four-bedroom home. This is where he took me, telling me I could stay as long as I wanted. "Get freshened up and then meet me in the courtyard to talk business."

I showered and shaved and walked out in the blazing Italian sunshine, wearing the ridiculous Italian jumpsuit that had been laid out on my bed; I didn't want to offend. The air was fragrant with the scent of fresh-tilled earth and sunbaked vineyards. Uncle Louie was reading a newspaper at a beat-up table in the courtyard, in the shade. There was a bottle of wine on the table, no label, and two tiny glasses. When he saw me, he poured and held a glass to me.

"We got the contacts," he said. "We can make it happen. But first . . . *saluti.*"

We cheered and drank. I wasn't much of a red-wine guy. For all the money and glamor, I was still that poor surfer kid from Redondo Beach, so the wine tasted like sour ass to me. But I didn't let on. "It's fantastic," I lied. "Notes of . . . is that plum?" It was slightly tangy yet sweet, and the only fruit that came to mind.

He clapped his hands. "Very good, Owen! Very good." He drained his glass and encouraged me to as well.

"I got a group o' guys, a syndicate out of Amsterdam. They got people in Australia who are constantly purchasing cocaine. They'll buy your product. So if you're for real. . ."

"I'm definitely for real."

He didn't yet believe that I had people who could move coke into the country. It was still the Holy Grail of cocaine. It would take a total fucking madman to want to smuggle it into Australia. But he was also hopeful because he badly needed cash. He had IRS problems back in the States, which is why he now spent most of his time abroad even though he was a dual citizen. Back in his heyday, he had been *the* guy who trafficked marijuana from Southern California to the East Coast, where he sold to the Lucchese family in New York and New Jersey. He also trafficked coke from Colombia to the U.S. and Amsterdam. He was rolling in the dough. But something happened, I'm not sure what. A mistake, a tiny misstep, and it all came crashing down. Maybe he fucked the wrong guy's wife. Maybe he got pinched, or someone narced on him. Whatever the case, it seemed he lost everything but his various homes and a modest savings account. He decided to cash in his chips, thank his lucky stars he wasn't serving thirty-five to life, and just enjoy his quietude with his family in Italy. But once you taste that lifestyle, that high, it's impossible to go back to normal. The more he talked about the possibilities, the more I could see it in his speech and his mannerisms. He was excited—manic, even. He kept saying this was a once-in-a-lifetime opportunity. That if we managed to pull this off, we'd become multi-millionaires overnight.

But what he said next chilled me to the bone. "It's either that . . . or prison."

A shiver of fear came over me. I shook it off and raised my glass. "No prison. Just millions."

Back in L.A., I texted El Jefe excitedly, telling him about my trip to Italy and that I had an Amsterdam crew ready to buy whatever product he needed, using their satellite operation in Australia. I was a little disappointed with his response. "We need a better plan. You must have a legitimate reason to be in Australia."

Right. I was brand new to the cocaine smuggling world, and this felt like a dumb oversight on my part. Of course I'd need a legit reason. I thought up scenarios, ultimately deciding I'd go to a restaurant-management school in Sydney. This is something I wanted to get into anyway down the line, once the money started piling up. I might as well kill two birds with one stone. I flowed the idea to El Jefe, and he responded with one word: "Perfect."

I had somewhat of an alibi, too. My aunt lived in Perth, so I'd make sure to drop in and visit her as often as I could. El Jefe agreed to cover all expenses, including the ten grand for the school. It all felt too surreal. The cartel was enrolling me in restaurant-management school in Australia, and I was about to start smuggling millions of dollars of cocaine. It was laughable, really. But it was also fucking terrifying. There were a thousand things that could go wrong, and, being the middleman, I was either liable to piss off the Mexican drug cartel, or I was going to piss off the Italian gangster with mob connections worldwide. I wondered if there was a secret contract I'd just signed with them. Had I just agreed to forfeit my life if, say, the shipment gets picked up by border control? What if Uncle Louie fucks me, and by association the cartel? He did keep going on about how "we" would become multi-millionaires virtually overnight. Maybe that was his meal ticket; he'd keep all the cash himself, my cut and El Jefe's, and launder it into some offshore account so he could be set for life. No, he'd taken me to meet his family. I'd stayed at his *home*. There was no way he'd screw me. And he'd been in the business long enough to know that the basic rule on this earth was you did not fuck with the cartel.

The plan started running quickly. Uncle Louie and I were to fly to Australia and get ourselves a couple of apartments, where we'd stay for a few months. I'd enroll in school, start classes, visit the aunt in Perth. Everything was aboveboard. When the time came, I'd oversee receiving the cocaine through mail couriers. I'd hand the coke over to Uncle Louie, and he would then sell it. The money would then be given to me, and I would have to find a way to transfer El Jefe's cut to him. I was getting $50,000 per kilo from the cartel; our agreement was that anything we made, we split. I was going to sell the kilos to Uncle Louie for $100,000, and he would sell them wholesale to his people for $150,000. Everybody wins.

I headed to Australia a few weeks later and settled into my apartment. I started attending classes in an all-brick four-story building off George Street, the opposite side of town from my apartment. Classes were made up mostly of international students like myself, all of them chasing the dream of opening up their own hotel or restaurant some day. I suppose I was too, the only difference being that it would be funded and perhaps even overseen by the cartel. I was careful to keep a low profile. I wasn't here to make friends or have any sort of reputation: I was here for business.

Pretty soon after my arrival, I oversaw my first deal. El Jefe wanted to do a smaller test run of ten kilos just to make sure it was all legit. I was contacted by a DHL driver via my encrypted phone, who told me to book a room at the local Four Seasons. As soon as I checked in, he wanted me to text him the room number. I was standing, waiting inside the room, pacing, when I heard a knock at the door. It was the driver, in uniform. He came in and shut the door, then handed me the package, told me to count them and verify that all ten were there.

I opened the package and, sure as shit, there were ten kilos of pure Colombian cocaine, all with a sparkly fish-scale flair and a scorpion stamped on the front of each brick. I hefted the package, the weight of a dumbbell, idly realizing that I was holding a million dollars in my hands. I thought about sticking a pocketknife in there and giving myself a bump like they do in the movies, but the driver would probably laugh at me. He was one of El Jefe's, after all, and they knew what they were doing. The coke was real. It was for the buyers to do the movie shit.

Uncle Louie came in several minutes later. His eyes were huge, a mix of fear and excitement mottling his dark brows. "You have it?" I showed him. He beamed, putting the package into a travel suitcase. "They're here. I will be right back," he said.

I felt strangely powerless at this juncture of the transaction. I'd just handed over a million bucks of drugs to a guy I barely knew; a million bucks of the *cartel's* coke, I should say. I did not know if Uncle Louie had a gambling addiction or was an alcoholic or sex addict, or maybe he suffered from a mental disorder. I did not know if he had any major debts. I guess this is what you call blind faith.

Uncle Louie left, and twenty minutes later he rolled two black suitcases, containing a million dollars in cash, into the room. He was sweating profusely and smelled of body odor, probably the nerves. He reeked. "When can we do the next round?" he asked excitedly.

"Holy shit," is all I could muster. The entire transaction had been completed within half an hour. "How am I going to count all this money?" It was like staring at a massive trove of monopoly money. I had to be sure it was the right amount; El Jefe would want me to double-check. I went down to a jewelry shop in Chinatown and saw a guy counting bills in a money machine. "Where do I get me one of those?" I asked.

He shrugged. "I could sell you one."

"How much?"

"$350."

I paid the money and hauled ass back to my apartment. I started counting the cash, but the fucking machine kept jamming up. It couldn't handle all the money. I marched back to the jeweler and placed the thing back on the counter. "Hey, man, this thing is garbage. It keeps jamming."

"Oh? How much money are you counting?"

"A lot."

"Sorry, I didn't realize how much you were . . . listen, I got an associate down the street who can help you out. He can sell you the best one, banker quality."

I did as he said, paid a grand to his guy and went back to my apartment. I felt like a kid on Christmas morning, sitting in my empty kitchen and counting all the cash. But that feeling of child-like anticipation quickly faded to stress and anxiety. It took three hours to count it all and put rubber bands on the stacks properly. As I was counting, I kept thinking what if I fuck up and have to start all over again? What if Uncle Louie's crime syndicate had shorted me: Would I get whacked for that? It would be so easy for someone like me to take a few stacks, maybe forty or fifty grand, and keep it for myself, blaming it on the buyers. I wondered what El Jefe's protocol was for this. Surely they had been through it before. Did they whack the buyers, the sellers, both? Or maybe they made both parties pay up regardless of who had pinched the money.

I calmed myself down. The money was all there. I had this.

I messaged El Jefe on the Phantom Secure phone. "I've got your money, boss. Everything went off without a hitch."

"Very good."

"What do you want me to do with it?"

"Hang on to it."

"Hang on to it?"

"Yes, we'll deal with that later. When are you ready for the next shipment?"

"We're ready."

And that was that. A few days later I handled a shipment of twenty kilos this time, two million dollars. It was a fuck ton of cash. Uncle Louie was freaking out, as all the cupboards in our apartments were stacked to the tits with money. We didn't even have any dishes. You'd open a cupboard to grab the coffee and a half million bucks would come spilling out. We were both a little nervous. How in the hell could we get this much money out of the country?

Uncle Louie said he'd go to Switzerland to his banking contacts and figure out how to launder his money. The drug business was every man for himself, I realized. I was in charge of mine and El

Jefe's money, which might just be the most important role I played in the whole operation. No wonder El Jefe had tapped me for this; he'd been impressed with the million cash I moved from Texas to California. That was all down to my contacts and a little bit of luck; but I was in Australia now, and I had jack shit for contacts. I had to get creative.

As the cash was piling up, Uncle Louie and I were getting more nervous. We had been told by his Amsterdam contacts that the biker gangs in Australia—Hell's Angels, The Mongols, The Rebels—if they found out you were moving any sort of product that they didn't get a percentage of, you'd get whacked. Disappeared. Just like that. And we would really have to look the part and blend in with the rest of the guys in the business district to not raise suspicion. We wore two-piece suits and Ferragamo shoes and wheeled our cash around in suitcases. But the stress was taking its toll. We were drinking in the mornings, popping Xanax and bumps of coke to calm our nerves. It was ironic; as more money kept piling up, the more anxious we became. Because how the fuck were we going to get it out of the country?

At the same time, my girlfriend Desiree had been hitting me up. She was the gorgeous Latina girl I had met in Las Vegas five months before. We had been messaging back and forth, and I let her in on my dilemma, with some details excluded. She knew I was in the gambling business, so I stuck with that. "Babe, I've got a lot of gambling money, a few million, and I have no idea how to get it back to the States."

"How much?" she asked.

"A bit over three million."

"*En serio*, Owen?"

I hesitated. Five months of dating. But this chick was on the level, a fucking boss. The best girl I'd ever dated. She'd been born in

Mazatlán, Sinaloa, home of Don Neto, El Mayo, and El Chapo, the original gangsters of Mexico, so I knew she must have contacts from her family who still lived in the fishing town of Sinaloa. I could trust her. "It's not exactly . . . uh, *legal*," I told her.

The pause on the other end of the line had my heart racing.

"I know someone," she said in Spanish. "This gambler from Vegas who plays blackjack. He's really good and he plays with a lot of money. Maybe he can help you wash it. But you'll need to get back here ASAP and meet with him. I'll arrange it. His name is RJ Cipriani, and he goes by Robin Hood."

"All right, babe. But don't give him my real name. Tell him I go by Junior."

I thought it was worth a try. What else was I going to do? I told El Jefe I was heading back to the States so I could get a jump on getting the money back there, asking if it was okay that we put this on hold. He seemed a little surprised. "Sure, but we have a lot more product to move."

I promised I'd have it all figured out within a week. So I put three million bucks in my bathroom attic above the toilet, half of which was mine, and hopped on a plane to Los Angeles to meet this gambler, Cipriani.

CHAPTER 5

The Fairmont Hotel on Ocean Boulevard, one block from the boardwalk and the white sands of Santa Monica beach. A hulking rectangular edifice, behind giant swaying palms and a massive old fig tree the size of a whole city block.

Dressed in a two-piece suit, I strode into the café past the lobby and spotted Cipriani immediately. He had a long face, an Italian nose, and a chin that jutted out like a bulldog's. He was wearing sunglasses and a baseball cap. I nodded to him, he nodded back, and I walked over to his table and extended my hand. "Junior," I said.

"RJ."

I took a seat and got straight to business. "I'm a bookie from right here in L.A., but I've got an absolute whale of a customer in Sydney, Australia, who owns a bunch of textile businesses and wants to play with his cash over there. But he's down."

"Down how much?"

He kept glancing around, paranoid, his hat pulled far down on his face.

"Three million. But rumor has it he's got close to twenty mil to bet with me."

RJ was quiet a long moment. He took a quick nervous sip from his cocktail, again glancing around. He sniffled. I wondered if he had imbibed prior to our meeting. "You need a way to get it out."

"Yes. Back to Beverly Hills. If you're interested, what would be your fee, and how would you do it?"

RJ nodded eagerly. "Let's start with a smaller amount, maybe $1.5 million. Here's what we'll do. I'll go to the casino down there, a sister casino to the Palazzo and Venetian out of Vegas called the Star Casino. I'll have my host call and say something like 'Hey, there's a VIP whale coming into town wanting to play at your casino. He'll have north of $3 million, but I don't know how long he'll want to play as he's always traveling.' The plan is, I'll go in and play with the $1.5 million in casino chips, then act bored. I'm just not feeling it, you know? So I'll pull the host aside and say this and ask to cash out my chips. Being a whale, they'll do whatever I ask. They'll issue me a check, which I'll take back to Vegas and cash out at the Venetian. Easy. Just like that. Minus my 25 percent fee."

I couldn't believe just how quickly this guy launched into the perfect way to launder money. As if he had done this before. And 25 percent? That was kind of bold, given that his only job was to fly into Australia all expenses paid and just sit and play well for an hour and cash out what was left. But if he was as good a gambler as people said, and he could stand to play with that sum of cash without blowing through it all, then he was worth every bit of that 25 percent to El Jefe and therefore to me.

The only question now—the most important question of all in this business—was: Could he be trusted? I watched as he kept glancing around, his head on a swivel. Was he in trouble with somebody? What did he expect to happen, some gangsters to blow through the fucking Fairmont and shoot him up? He came vetted from my girlfriend, but I'd have to find out more. For the moment, the deal was sound.

"How soon can you get started?" I said.

"How soon do you need me?"

"As soon as you can."

He shrugged. "I'll be there next week, then."

We shook hands.

Cipriani, in addition to the 25 percent take, insisted that I get him first-class tickets to Australia that included a bed, which came to around $25k roundtrip. Preferably Virgin Australia or Qantas Airlines. He said this as I was about to get up, just to make sure the deal was sound.

He also said "I want the best hotel in Sydney. Penthouse. Book it for four nights." That was another ten grand. I paid for our drinks when the waiter came over. He didn't thank me. "And what kind of suitcases do you use, you know, for the cash?"

"I've been using Swapmeet suitcases," I said, putting my wallet back in my jacket. They only cost a couple hundred bucks and were good enough for the job. But Cipriani shook his head like I was a complete amateur.

"No. I will *only* accept cash in a Tumi roller. They're carbon fiber, and I need to make sure it's strong enough to wheel the $1.5 up to the casino cage without it keeling over or me looking like an idiot carrying a case full of dumbells. The knockoff brands won't do the job, so don't bring that bullshit. Tumi. Only."

I was a bit taken aback, for two reasons. Not only was he experienced, but arrogant too. "Is that all?" I said, painfully withholding the "your majesty" at the end. I watched him drink his cocktail sourly, kind of wishing I'd not agreed to the 25 percent.

"No. I need a throwaway registered in no one's name. We'll use it to communicate. Make sure you've got a phone number nobody else has used. Just us. All right?"

I walked away from that meeting and immediately called Desiree. "Holy shit, babe."

"What?"

"This guy's higher maintenance than *you*!"

She laughed. "It's because he's the real deal."

I climbed into my Range Rover. "I fucking hope so. Because if he doesn't pull through, I'm screwed on all his expenses alone."

Before Cipriani came to Australia, I'd been finding my own creative ways to launder the money. I had to. I couldn't let it keep piling up, or else I'd have had nowhere to fucking sit in my apartment.

I called my best friend from college, Levi—a loan officer who owned his own mortgage company—and asked him to come to Australia with his accountant brother Duke and his father-in-law to help me clean some cash. The only way I could do it was if I had some more people with fake IDs going to currency exchanges to trade the Australian dollars for U.S. dollars or euros. He said "Sure, buddy."

I flew all three of them first class to Sydney, put them up at the Four Seasons, and then we hit the town. After wining and dining them, Duke said, "So what's the deal?"

"This rich Chinese client of mine, he keeps losing shitloads of cash on my gambling site. It's great for me, I'm swimming in his losses, but I can't move it all by myself. I can't get it back into the States legitimately. I need you guys to help me think of creative ideas."

Duke reached into his jacket pocket and brought out a bunch of passport cards. They were fraudulent, of course, multiples of all four of us with different identities. "These aren't very well known in Australia at the moment. A fake one won't look much different than a real one. And I've got a bunch more back at the hotel. I can make as many of these as you like, if that helps."

Duke told me that the Bank of China allowed you to bring $50,000 cash and wire it anywhere in the world without any bank account information. Between the four of us, we started wiring $200,000 a day at three different branches in Sydney. We wired the money to my shell corporations in the States and Costa Rica. Duke kept making fake IDs for us, giving me the name Junior DeLuca, which fit perfectly alongside my Italian "Uncle" Louie.

The underlying issue was that we could only do so much before they started recognizing our faces. The strategy was to rotate; we'd use a particular ID at each branch. So if I was Junior DeLuca at the George Street branch, I needed to remain Junior DeLuca there. If I was Tom Stanton at the Queens Street location, it stayed that way. The same with the other guys, and we only went once a week to keep from drawing attention to ourselves. It was slow going, and I found myself getting stressed again as texts from El Jefe came in. "When can we do the next shipment? We were off to a great start and now we're frozen. I do not like it." I reassured him I was doing everything I could on my end, washing hundreds of thousands a week. All I needed was our whale Cipriani to come to town, and he could do in a couple of hours what would take me and three other guys an entire month.

The Bank of China also let me set up a safety deposit box, so I started buying up a lot of gold bullion and storing it there as well. Pretty soon, Duke went back to San Diego to set up more shell corporations like a gold-bullion wholesaler and a diamond exchange, making it look legit for the wires coming in from the sale of my bullion. We would also go to the currency exchange, trade Australian currency for euros, then stash $20,000 in euros into comic books, put them into plastic comic book slips, seal them, slap Amazon stickers on, and ship these back to various P.O. boxes I had set up throughout Los Angeles.

Still, without Cipriani there yet, the process was daunting. Washing money was now my full-time job. I'd wake up in the morning, and on my agenda was: comic books, gold bullion and diamonds, and Bank of China. The glitz and glamor I had originally held for becoming a pony for the cartel was quickly wearing off, instead turning into boredom and tedious repetition. Then one day it dawned on me.

UGG boots.

They were from Australia, so they wouldn't look conspicuous being shipped to the States. I felt like Thomas Edison with his lightbulb. Like an insane person, I started buying up dozens of pairs of UGG boots. I'd go to the gold-bullion stores and buy one-ounce gold coins. The limit was $9,900 per day without an SMR (suspicious matter report) being filed, so I'd hit up all four bullion stores every day, take the soles out of the UGGs back at my apartment, and glue four one-ounce bullion coins to each UGG and put the sole back on them. Each pair I shipped to the States carried about twelve thousand dollars, and I started shipping a ton of them to friends and family. I'd call them up: "Hey, sis, what size UGG are you? You don't know? Well, I really need you to find out ASAP. Six, you think? Okay, great!" I told them to make sure they held on to the boots and I'd tell them why later, but it was very important. My dad, my mom, my college friends, old coworkers, everybody's girlfriends and wives, they all started getting the gift of UGGs in their mailboxes courtesy of good ol' Owen. And everybody thought I was fucking crazy.

I could imagine the conversations. "Why is Owen so obsessed with UGGs all of a sudden? Is he unwell?" I did get a few serious phone calls asking if I was having a quarter-life crisis. Had my girlfriend left me? Was I taking a new form of drug they hadn't heard of which made your obsessive tendencies go through the roof?

I laughed it off, just saying I was trying to respect the Australian tradition and loved it here so much, I wanted everyone I knew to have a piece of Australia. This process was still slow going, though. It took me an entire week to wash $200,000 through my UGGs. And it was a lot of fucking work.

Meanwhile, Duke was still setting up shell corporations left and right back in the U.S. He could set one up in under a minute at the computer, complete with a legit tax ID number and everything. He and his father-in-law tried to fly back to Australia to help me wash more money, but they got stopped at the Sydney airport during arrival screening. Border patrol took them to the hospital to x-ray their stomachs and see if they were bringing drugs into Australia.

"Why are you making such frequent trips to Australia?" they asked.

"We love this country and are thinking about emigrating here for business."

Border patrol agents searched their bags and found all their fake IDs. "And these?"

Duke was fucking slick. He played innocent. "We live right on the Mexican border. It's dangerous. Sometimes they kidnap Americans and hold them for ransom. We need to have different IDs." The agents ultimately let them go, but it was enough to spook us all and make us realize we needed to slow down before the whole operation was blown and we were tossed in prison for a long time. The idea of going to prison without even having gotten El Jefe his money was not a comfortable notion.

I needed Robin Hood.

A couple weeks after our meeting, Cipriani arrived in Sydney, well rested from his Qantas Airlines bed and complimentary Dom

Pérignon. He gave me a call from the Four Seasons penthouse I had booked him in, asking the plan, then met me at my apartment. I led him inside and opened the cabinets, stacks of cash piled to the brim and tipping over like Jenga towers. I had to quickly slam the cabinet shut before it all came piling out.

"Holy shit," he said. "You weren't lying."

"It's a lot, and more on the way. You stand to make a lot of dough with your 25 percent. How's the 1.5 for now, still doable?"

He waved his hand as if swatting an annoying fly. "Yeah, yeah, that's no problem. Let's get it in the suitcase."

I brought out one of the Tumi suitcases he'd personally requested and let several towers of cash flop out of the cabinet. I counted it out and put $1.5 million into the suitcase. Cipriani hefted it. "Not bad," he said. "Manageable."

We caught a cab back to his hotel and went with the suitcase up to his room. In front of the floor-to-ceiling windows, beyond which Sydney Harbor glimmered in the distance, Cipriani said "You know, I wanna do some good deeds and give some of the money to a poor family here. That kinda makes things look more legit, you know?"

At this point I had absolutely no idea how any of this worked. I didn't know how to launder money through gambling, that wasn't my forte. My only job in this whole exchange was to make sure El Jefe got his money at the end of the day. I didn't even want to think about the consequences if I didn't.

"Do whatever you gotta do," I said. "All I know is it's 1.5 minus the 25 percent you're going to charge me. If you can give me that, then we're clear. But I expect you to get that amount back to me."

This was business. And in business I'm a man of my word. I impressed upon him that this was important; if he said he was going to wash $1.5 million for me, I expected that $1.5 million washed and ready to be turned into a check. I had lied to him about who I was doing this for, but I knew if I told the Boss he was going to have his money, he damn well better have all of it.

Cipriani nodded. "Don't worry, I'm good at this. I'll make a little extra and skim that off the top. I got an interview with these 9News people that I'm giving back to a family in need."

"That's fine."

We parted ways. Cipriani headed to the Star Casino in Sydney with the Tumi suitcase full of cash. I'm sure he walked in like he had pineapples under his arms, his prominent chin jutted out and his head held high the way he always walked, a high-rolling East Coast guy. And I'm sure they gave him the royal treatment, rolled out the red carpet, constant bottle service. I didn't know if he drank much though. We had had cocktails, but he hadn't gone overboard. Aside from constantly looking around like the Feds were going to dip in at any moment, he seemed very confident and in control. I hoped I was right.

After two hours gambling at the Star Casino, up a hundred grand, Cipriani motioned to the host and said "Sorry, I'm just not feeling it. Would you cash me out?"

He called me from his throwaway phone and said the only two words I needed to hear. "It worked."

Turns out he had also told the host that he needed to go back to California, as somebody in his family was sick. "I've got a check here for $1.6 million," he told me.

I was ecstatic. Two hours. Christ. if I had him come here every two weeks, he could wash all the money I needed. No more comic books, no more UGGs, no more currency exchanges or Bank of China wire or bullion and diamond stores. I could start living again and just sell El Jefe's coke, which is what I was supposed to be doing anyway. This whole money-laundering thing was just a necessary hiccup: a natural impediment to a growing enterprise.

"What comes next?" I asked, excited.

"Well, that was the hard part: next comes the easy part. I go to the Venetian, they cash me in right there and I start playing again. Same routine, but I cash out in the U.S., and you have your money in U.S. dollars. I'm thinking it'll be done in two days."

I was floored. This guy really was the real deal. I didn't care about the arrogance anymore; I would rather he knew what he wanted than be unsure and make a mistake. He told me he had done this before too. Obviously the Tumi suitcases were important because of some experience he'd had. His methodology was tried and true. And it didn't hurt that he had the reputation of being a "Robin Hood," making donations with his winnings to people in need. His public profile was squeaky-clean and unquestionable. Who would suspect that *Robin Hood* was laundering money for the cartel? Well, to be fair, not Robin Hood, as he didn't know this. All he knew was that he was laundering for *me* and making that fat 25 percent. He didn't ask many questions once that figure was settled.

Two days after he secured the check from the Star Casino, he called me on a secure line, saying he had taken care of the money for me. He went up a little, then down a little, landing at just under a million dollars, five hundred grand short. "Don't worry," he assured me; "I'll make it up on the next one."

Because he was a whale, the casino let him cash out. He had $980,000 in cash and a private jet they supplied him back to L.A. "Where do you want the money?"

I was still in Australia at the time, laundering little bits of the other few million. I told him I didn't want him driving around with a million cash, so I instructed him to drop half a million with Desiree in one trip, then the other half to my old man. Neither had any idea it was drug money, they both thought it was just gambling money from my business. I then called a couple bookie friends and had them take the cash, convert it for a small percentage, and wire it to an offshore account in Costa Rica.

I proudly texted El Jefe. "The money's all washed and I have my new method worked out. I'm ready for the next shipment."

Now the fun was really going to start.

I wasn't the only one chomping at the bit to wash more money. Cipriani called me a week later. "I wanna do some more." I booked his tickets, and he was on his way.

I used my own take from the last few shipments to buy a house in a gated community in Costa Rica. The home had 360-degree views of the Pacific Ocean. Costa Rica was the nexus of my entire gambling operation, and that's where I could clean all my money, so it just made sense. Everything started coming together. And meanwhile El Jefe was shipping me forty kilos of coke at a time, which Uncle Louie promptly sold and handed me yet more suitcases filled with cash. I ran out of cabinet space so started storing millions of dollars in the attic above my bathroom that I mentioned before.

Cipriani showed up and I brought him $2.5 million in cash, two suitcases this time. He was impressed. "That's a lot."

"Can you manage it?"

He laughed. "Of course I can."

At a $625,000 take, I sure as hell hoped so.

"I'm going to spread it out over multiple casinos," he said. "I'll do a couple here, then go to Melbourne and play there. We can't wash all this at the Star Casino or they're definitely gonna notice."

Again, I said, "Whatever you gotta do."

At the time, I was investing in a rejuvenation center with my personal trainer. It had everything: lasers for fat reduction, Botox, fillers, testosterone, B12 shots. My money was starting to make me more money, and I couldn't have been happier. I was becoming a rich man, all the while my casino business was still flourishing. I was working out with this trainer when I got a call two days after I saw Cipriani. His voice was grim. "We got some problems," he said. My heart dropped.

My voice was low, measured, firm. "What kind of problems?"

"I, uh . . ." He paused. There was an eternity held in that pause, and I hated it. "I lost it all."

Any self-control was now gone. "What do you mean you fucking lost it all?"

He sounded nervous. "I'm only down to $300,000. I don't know, man. It's just bad luck. Bad luck."

"Bullshit you lost it all. It's been forty-eight hours. Listen, I'm at my office right now, off George Street. You need to come meet me someplace. I need to know what the hell is going on."

My trainer stared at me. "He's saying he lost $2.5 million?"

"Yes."

"Listen, I know a manager over at the Star Casino. Let's head over there, and he can pull up your guy's profile to see if he really lost the money or he's bullshitting you."

I nodded. "Meet me at the bar in the Star Casino at three."

My trainer Sean and I were dressed in three-piece suits, sitting at the bar in the Star Casino. All tatted up and on steroids, we probably looked pretty intimidating.

Cipriani showed up in a ball cap, sunglasses, baggy jeans, and a T-shirt, shaking like a leaf on a tree. He was sweating. He looked nervous. "Hi," he said, sitting down.

"We have some issues, man," I said flat-out. "You don't just lose $2.5 million of someone else's money."

Cipriani was speechless a few moments. He seemed terrified and perplexed. "It's just a bad run at the table."

"You stay here. My buddy and I are going to speak with the manager and pull up your profile to see if you really did lose it all."

Cipriani wasn't lying. I almost felt bad for him.

"No," the manager shook his head. "He didn't scam you. Guy came in with two suitcases full of cash and blew through it all."

I don't know if I was relieved. Cipriani was honest? That's all well and good, but it didn't bring back the two and a half million he lost. At least if he had skimmed the money, we could have gotten it back.

We went back to him. "I'm going to need you to bring me that $300k, and I'll need your passport. We've got to figure this out."

"No, no, I can make it back!" he pleaded. "I can make it all back. This is what I do, man."

"No. Bring the $300k, and bring your passport. You are not leaving this country until we figure out how to get that money back. It is not my money. There are some big guys out of New York and L.A. this money belongs to. I cannot lose this money."

————

Sean and I booked rooms at the Hilton on George Street for the meetup with Cipriani.

I poured us each a double tequila from the minibar, handed it to him. He thanked me with a nod and took a sip. I downed my drink in one gulp and poured another double. Behind me, the Sydney skyline was set afire as the sun descended below it. I watched as the dark consumed everything, that sinking feeling that my life was sinking with it like a curtain unfurling, a descent into a hellish place I was not familiar with, a place I couldn't navigate because I couldn't see.

On the table in front of me, my Phantom Secure phone buzzed, which could only mean one thing. Sean looked at me dubiously. I took a deep breath and another large gulp of tequila and massaged my temples. If I didn't answer the phone, I could keep that darkness at bay. An hour, three, an evening. Maybe I was out for the night on business, and I just came back in the morning? Nothing suspicious. The good news would be that I'd figured out the situation with Cipriani and I could tell the Boss that everything had gone off without a hitch. Cipriani was no pauper; he would simply have to pay up. Besides, he already had me out five hundred grand from the last wash and promised he would make it up. Now we were out three million dollars. He lived in a multi-million-dollar condo right on Santa Monica Beach. He was a fucking whale, for Christ's sake, known the world over as a high-stakes blackjack player. He gambled with me on this laundering business, and he lost. The common law of gambling was that you paid your debt. I don't give a damn if it's your pension or your retirement or your trust fund. You pay that shit because that is the common law of exchange. You want something, you pay for it. You lose something in a game of risk, you pay for that too. It's the main principle of society: fucking pay me.

Another buzz. Another drink. Another massage to my temples and the dire wish for this to all go away with one simple knock at the door, that arrogant jutted chin and dark sunglasses, a check in his hand for three million bucks and maybe even a humble apology.

Another buzz.

I waited. There was no knock at the door.

"You gonna get that, O?" Sean asked. He watched me carefully. He knew what business I was in. Knew if you got three texts on your Phantom Secure in rapid succession, it could not have been good news.

Sighing, I finished my drink and grabbed the phone. It was El Jefe, of course.

How's it going with the $2.5 million? he asked.

I would really like to start moving product again.

Can we do 50 kilos this week? Tell me how the 2.5 went.

I groaned. "Fuck." Nearly a whisper. The breath had been wrenched from my lungs.

"Your boss?" Sean asked.

I shook my head. "Not my boss. *The* boss."

Sean was silent a moment. "What happens if you. . ." He hesitated. I already knew what he was going to ask; I'd been thinking of it myself all day long. "What happens if you can't pony up the three million?"

"I think you know."

Sean shrugged. This wasn't his business, after all. I held a finger gun to my head and fired. He winced and looked away. Very little consolation you could give to a dead man.

I texted El Jefe. "My guy said he would be all done by tomorrow morning. Feel free to send the product next week and I'll move it."

There had to be a solution to all this, even if Cipriani didn't pull through. Wasn't it obvious? I was making 50 percent alongside the boss. That's a huge cut. I would tell El Jefe my guy fucked up and lost the money, so I'd be working for free and at interest until the $3 million was paid off. At this rate, with fifty kilos coming in, that would be in a week's time, maybe two. The outstanding issue was I'd again have to figure out how to wash all the money and get it to him, as clearly this gambler had no fucking clue what he was doing. Fifty kilos was five million. My cut would be $2.5 million, the same amount this fake "Robin Hood" asshole had just lost. I'd give my cut to El Jefe with interest, and before that I'd wire him $500k of my own savings in good faith to make up for the $500k Cipriani had lost the last time. I got this. I could fix it after all. The numbers were sound, and the plan would work.

But then came the phone call.

"We uh . . . we got a problem," Cipriani said. His voice was trembling. I wanted to scream.

"What kind of problem?"

He was in a car, driving. Traffic sounds. "The cops are on me."

"Why the fuck would the cops be on you?"

"I don't know, man, but they are. They've been following me."

I shook my head. He's just being paranoid, like at the Fairmont where we met. "Listen, man, just come to the Hilton. You're fine; the cops aren't following you. Room 1326, all right? Get here as soon as you can. We need to figure this out."

As I hung up the phone, Sean stared at me. "Do you think he's gonna make it?" he said.

"He fucking better."

But the anxiety was eating me alive. What if the cops *were* on his tail? This motherfucker was up to some shady business, had to be if he was already so well-versed in the art of money laundering. Maybe he pulled this shit on somebody back in L.A., some powerhouse in organized crime. A $5 million loss and the guy wanted his money back, which was why Cipriani had kept glancing around at the Fairmont, his head on a swivel just waiting for something to go down. He was pale and was wearing sunglasses. Had he been holed up in some nondescript hotel for God knows how long, waiting out whatever threat he was running from? Maybe the client got fed up and framed him for something. Planted a few kilos in his condo and called the cops. Put out the APB, and Interpol was notified Cipriani was in Australia.

The possibilities were endless, and all bad. I decided that before our meeting with Cipriani, we should head back to my apartment and grab a bunch of cash just in case. Because he knew where I lived, and all the money was there. We went and packed $700k in a suitcase and I gave it to Sean. "Take this to your room at the Hilton. I'll meet you in an hour. Call me if Cipriani shows up before me and just keep him there, don't let him leave. Get his passport."

After an hour, I got in a taxi and called Sean. No answer. A weird feeling came over me; he always answers. I went back inside and kept blowing him up, pacing my apartment until two in the morning, until finally a female answered. "Who is this?" she said, pure business. She sounded like a cop.

"Junior DeLuca. I'm calling to get in touch with Sean Carolyn."

"Sean Carolyn is in custody right now. Can you tell me about the $700,000 found on his person?"

Fuck. Panic. Run.

"No, I don't know anything about that. I'm sorry."

I hung up the phone.

And the dark descended.

Days later, Sean and I were at the office of our new lawyer, the pieces slowly coming together.

Apparently, in a bid to save his own ass, Cipriani called the cops. He assumed we had guns on us, so he called this Hilton, saying "There's a gun in room 1326." We didn't have any guns. What we did have was a rolling suitcase with $700,000 of El Jefe's money. Cipriani was worried we were gonna whack him, which was the dumbest shit I ever heard. Why would I want to kill the guy who owes me three million dollars? Would the three million magically appear in the wake of his death? Was I in his will all of a sudden? This was probably from his own personal experience as a slimeball.

Suddenly, the image of him glancing all around the Fairmont made perfect sense.

When Sean arrived at the Hilton, four police officers were there to greet him.

"Are you Sean Carolyn?"

"Yes."

The rolling suitcase by his side probably suddenly felt like a death sentence.

"We got a call that there's a gun in your room."

He shook his head. "Are you sure you got the right room? I don't have any guns in there. I don't even own firearms."

"We know. We checked."

Sean waited.

"Is the gun in the bag?"

"No. I told you I don't own any firearms. This must be a mistake."

"What's in the bag?"

"Sorry, that's none of your business. And I haven't done anything wrong."

"You might as well tell us, because we're searching it either way."

"It's money from an investor of mine. I'm building a weight-loss clinic down the road right off George Street, and he's investing in the business. I'm a personal trainer."

"Right. Please step aside, sir."

Sean complied, and an officer went and opened the bag, revealing it filled to the brim with cash. They immediately took him in and started questioning him. He stuck to his story. "It's just money from my business partner, Junior DeLuca. He's investing with me in the weight-loss center I told you about." This was partially true, but I was investing a quarter million, not $700k. And typically you didn't invest in businesses with nearly a million cash.

Sean got released within a day, but he had a court date and the cops held onto the cash. So now I was out nearly four million bucks. Our new lawyer sat behind his desk, tapping a pen on the surface. "We can get that money back," he said. "We can pay people for that."

Again, I was pacing the room, high on coke and half drunk at ten in the morning. I was a fucking basket case. *Four million dollars, gone. What was I going to tell El Jefe?* The night of Sean's arrest, I'd taken every bit of cash from my apartment and put it in a storage unit, then wiped clean any indication I'd ever been there and left the place with the key on the table. The cops would now be looking for Junior DeLuca, so I found myself acting as paranoid as that asshole Robin Hood, who was probably long gone by now.

"How?" I demanded. "How do we get the money back?"

"We just need to come up with a story about who you are and where this money came from. I know the right barrister. We'll pay him and get that cash back to you guys. But you need to tell me . . . where did it come from?"

I shrugged. "It's just gambling money. I own an online gambling business. It's legit."

"Isn't that illegal in the States?"

"It's not in the States: the servers are all offshore in Costa Rica, totally legal and legit."

The lawyer nodded. "Then we can figure this out. Just give me a week or two."

There was no way I was waiting around for a week or two. After the meeting, I went straight to the airport and booked a flight back to L.A. Walking through the airport, it felt reminiscent of the first time I'd smuggled performance-enhancing drugs across the Mexican border when I was twenty-one. The drugs taped to my leg, the adrenaline, the fear. Only this time I was smuggling hundreds of kilos and laundering millions of dollars for a notorious drug king-pin. Would the police know what I looked like by now? They would be looking for Junior DeLuca. I wore a ball cap and sunglasses just like Cipriani. I half expected to see him on my flight, but I didn't. I slugged martinis like I was going to die tomorrow, because in all likelihood I probably would. I went over my response to El Jefe again and again. "My guy lost all the money, got spooked when I arranged a meetup, and called the cops on us saying we had a gun. My business partner got picked up, but nobody knows who I am and I have no association to it, aside from the $700k the cops picked up, which our lawyer says we will definitely get back. I'm going to figure this all out and get your money back to you ASAP. The rest of the money is in storage and safe."

Sending this message was like admitting to your wife that you'd cheated. No, way worse. It was putting your head on the chopping block, looking up at the hooded executioner, and saying "Go ahead. I'm ready."

I sent the text the morning after Sean got arrested. I had never been more scared in my entire life, the seconds ticking by with the slowness of a mountain being ground down over millennia.

"Get back to America. We will chat then."

What the fuck did that even mean? Was he coming to the States to personally put a bullet in my head?

The lawyer got ahold of me right after I touched down in L.A. "I've got an idea," he said.

He had this concert promoter friend of his, Andrew McManus, who promoted famous bands like Fleetwood Mac and ZZ Top. This guy agreed to say he'd borrowed the $700k from me back in the U.S. to arrange for the band to come out to Australia and play a few shows, giving the cash to their manager. The deal was I'd get the $700k back in Australia plus a percentage of the ticket sales. The cash in the bag was just the initial loan.

"What about Sean saying it was for an investment in his business?"

"Don't worry about it, we'll just say Sean made a mistake."

"So what's going to happen?"

"I'll tell the coppers this story and they'll just request an interview with you. You got to make sure you stick to the story. I'll give you names, dates, details, et cetera. It'll work."

"I am not going back to Australia."

"You don't have to. You can do an interview at any police station near you. It'll be within the next few months. Don't worry, we've got it figured out."

CHAPTER 6

No sooner had I gotten on the tarmac in Los Angeles than I received a text from El Jefe.

I now looked at my Phantom Secure phone as if it were a loaded gun prone to misfire. You handle it in just the wrong way and it blows your fucking head off. Or maybe a hunk of molten steel; you pick it up, and it scorches the flesh off your palm, burning straight through the bone and marrow of your hand. I physically trembled as I held it. Bringing it to my face, I leaned against a wall past the jet bridge in LAX, all the passengers drifting by in an endless procession, checking their phones, telling their spouses they touched down safely and will be home soon, reassuring their parents, and checking in on the kids. And here I was, slowly opening my phone to the death knell of El Jefe's text: "What's going on, Owen? I haven't heard from you."

Obviously, I couldn't lie. That would certainly make me a dead man. What was my recourse now? I had none, I realized. As soon as I'd learned from the lawyer that the feds were actively searching for my alias Junior DeLuca, I knew it was only a matter of time before they found Owen Hanson. I could never go back to Australia, which meant my idea—to just keep selling the Boss's product and give him my cut and then some until he was paid off—was moot. With no recourse, I was forced to ask myself the most difficult question since all this began: What use was I to him now?

In Australia, I could handle millions of dollars in product each week. Here in America, I was just like any other two-bit drug dealer. I had no magic sauce here. I wasn't even experienced in the drug trade, not on this level. I ran an online gambling operation, which did well for me, but I saw no way El Jefe could get in on that in any wildly profitable way. Or maybe this was my atonement; I hand over all my gambling accounts to El Jefe and his associates, and I walk away from the whole thing. Start a brand-new life. A poor man, but not a dead man. This gave me some modicum of hope.

"*Viejon*, I need to see you in person. The shit went south, but I'm going to fix it. I really feel it's best if I come see you. Can we meet in person?"

"Let's meet in Baja tomorrow. I'll fly in with *mis plebes* to the private airport. One of my drivers will pick you up from the McDonald's on the Mexican side once you cross the San Ysidro bridge. From there we will have a sit-down at my favorite restaurant near Rosarito Beach. Be at the McDonald's at one p.m. sharp."

Beads of sweat formed at my temples, slid down my cheeks.

His soldiers? Pick me up? Across the border, away from the laws and protection of my country? Fuck me. This must be how Cipriani felt about coming to the hotel room and giving me his passport, but a hundred times worse. I was heading straight into the fucking lion's den. And unlike him, I was no coward but a man of my word. I would never rat on El Jefe. I had known what I was getting into, and if it got fucked up, that was on me. I would face the consequences and plead my case the best I could, even if that meant a bullet in my head.

The next morning, I donned my most comfortable golf slacks, Gucci loafers, and a Lululemon T-shirt. If I was gonna die, it would be in style with dignity and courage. Admittedly, the elephant's dose of Oxycontin, Xanax, and Norco helped, as well as the whole

Xanibar I'd taken the night before, washed down with a shot of Patron. Self-medicated to the extreme, I climbed into my Range Rover like I was slipping into the ether of a lucid dream, all the lights too bright, the road sounds dulled, the reality of this whole experience suspended and immaterial and blurred.

I parked at a Jack in the Box at the border and texted El Jefe: "I'm parked, about to walk over the bridge now to the McDonald's." Again, that sensation, the awful nagging voice in my head worse than ever before: *"You dumb bastard, you're walking headlong toward your own death. Each step farther from here on is one step closer to the bullet that has your name on it. He's probably in his armory right now, selecting the perfect weapon. Maybe not a gun, maybe something slow and intimate, a knife or a screwdriver, jumper cables. Maybe all the above? Regardless, you're a dumb bastard, and you did this to us. We could have had a great run if not for you. You should have listened to me more. Now we're dead."*

My hands squeezing the steering wheel so tightly my knuckles were blanched white, I tried to kill the voice. But the voice remained.

A buzz on the phone. Checked it. "My guys will be there."

"You've got five minutes to turn the car around and head back. Save your life. For Christ's sake, Owen! SAVE US!"

I smacked myself. Again. Again. Took a few deep breaths. No, I will not die today. I will give El Jefe all my businesses, all my assets. Fuck, maybe I'll just be an indentured servant for the rest of my life. But I won't act desperate and scared, I'll act cool and respectful. It'll all be just f—

"YOU'RE GONNA FUCKING DIE, OWEN!"

Goddammit!

Another smack. The pain felt good, like a cool burst of wind on a scorching day, which it was, the desert plains on both sides of the car stretching endlessly, omnipotent and foreboding. A man could walk a hundred miles in that desert and not see a single soul. He could die out there and be forgotten, his bones collecting dust for decades.

This was the most common trapping of power and wealth. Like a king, the more you acquire, the more people want to take it from you, go to war against you, stab you in the back like Brutus against Caesar and take every last thing you've got: your home, family, wealth—and ultimately your life. This was the price you paid for power. But the worst part was when you went to war with yourself, your own mind fighting against you. No. I was stronger than that. That voice in my head could go fuck itself.

I walked across the bridge and waited at the McDonald's. At 1:00 p.m. on the dot, a bulletproof black Escalade came into view. It slowed, turned around, and sidled up next to me. The passenger-side window slid down. A Mexican man wearing sunglasses nodded his head to the back and said "*Güero*," which meant "fair-skinned kid." I walked toward the car, each measured step carrying the weight of oblivion behind it, the sun impossibly bright, the wind rough and hot. The door opened for me, revealing two *sicarios* holding AK-47s.

I slipped into the back seat. In Spanish, I said "Good afternoon, gentlemen. My name is Owen."

They nodded, said nothing. We pulled out onto the road.

Ten minutes later, a bulletproof black Hummer and two trucks showed up in the rearview. The driver noticed and pulled over. What the fuck was happening?

"The Boss just arrived," the driver said in Spanish. Private plane in Tijuana airport's exclusive section. I wondered where El Jefe had come from, but no sooner did the thought strike than a group of men with automatic weapons emerged from the trucks, militant and on watch, glancing up and down the road. One of the sicarios came to the driver's side and said something hastily in Spanish. He spoke fast: all I caught was "Puerto Nuevo number one," probably the address of the restaurant. The driver nodded and proceeded. The motorcade fell in line behind us. Surreally, it reminded me of the last time I had been in a motorcade nearly a decade ago with the Trojans headed to the Pro Player Stadium in Miami Gardens for the Orange Bowl. The situations couldn't have been any more different. Back then, we'd had a fifty-man police escort delivering us to the most momentous occasion of my life. Now I was being guided by *sicarios* of the cartel to what was likely the end of my life.

Eventually we pulled up at a deserted restaurant. There were no cars in the lot but one, a beat-up old jalopy. There were no buildings, people, or vehicles in sight, as if we'd just entered a ghost town along the cold desert plains of the Midwest. We got out, and I felt strangely sanguine in the face of all this inherent danger. My whole life had led up to this moment. I had put myself here; nobody else had. I had made the decisions that led to the next moment, and the next, and the next, until ultimately I arrived at a deserted restaurant in Mexico among a coterie of armed guards and a drug kingpin. Was it my upbringing? The lack of a family unit and the loss of my mom and sister so young? Or was it Owen fucking Hanson? I knew with total clarity it was the latter. *I* had done this. I was responsible. And now, I had acceptance for that fact. I had made my bed. And it was time to take the long sleep.

"Inside," one of the armed guards said. There were ten of them. I saw El Jefe climb out of the Hummer. Cartier gold sunglasses matched his rose gold Yacht Master Rolex. He wore a fitted Versace T-shirt along with True Religion jeans, his black Versace loafers kicking up small clouds of dust as they padded toward me, several *sicarios* flanking him. He stood at 5'7", but looked bigger, his muscular arms squeezing past the confines of his shirtsleeves, probably on some sort of testosterone therapy. He sported a five o'clock shadow.

He approached me smiling, his hand extended.

"*Güero*, pleasure to finally meet you." He told me his name. A name I will not ever repeat.

We were led inside. It was empty, aside from a cook and a waiter. He must have bought out the entire joint. I asked if I could use the restroom and got a curt nod. In the bathroom, I took a swig of GHB and ate half a Xanax bar. My nerves were shot, and the voice in the back of my head had taken the reins to the extreme. *"DEAD MAN DEAD MAN DEAD MAN!"*

I needed a cocktail. Three. Ten. As soon as I sat down with the Boss, I asked if that was possible. "Of course," he said calmly, waving his hand at the waiter, who came immediately and took our drink orders. I asked for a margarita, real heavy on the tequila. A quadruple if possible. El Jefe ordered a beer and lobster for the table. When my drink arrived at the table, again almost instantly, I could tell it was almost all tequila. The waiter probably knew what I knew: it was my last day on Earth; I might as well be a little drunk for it.

The Boss said "Owen, tell me. What happened in Australia?"

I broke down the whole thing. Cipriani, the successful first wash, the extreme promise of the second. Then asshole Robin Hood's fuckup and cowardice, calling the cops reporting a gun that didn't exist, me trying to put out the fire and protect the rest of the money, but once again that failing miserably and the loss of the final $700k and Sean's arrest. I assured El Jefe we already had a plan to get that money back, and the remaining few million that was in my apartment was all in a safe place and ready for pickup, in addition to gold bullion and diamonds. He listened, calm and conciliatory. I noticed he did not take a sip of his drink; what kind of Mexican was he? That beer should have been gone by now. He was testing me, trying to read me. When I'd finished, he responded simply: "You know the old Pablo Escobar saying that goes like this, *Güero*: '*Plata o plomo.*'"

I knew exactly what this meant. A cartel term.

He seemed very serious now. "Do you know what this means, Owen?"

I nodded. "Yes, I do, sir." I took a huge gulp from my drink.

"Tell me. What does it mean?"

"It means: Money or lead."

He was saying you either pay, or you're going to get killed.

El Jefe nodded. "That is correct. It's one or the other, as you Americans say."

"I have no issue paying you back. I pull in those kinds of numbers with my gambling business. As far as I'm concerned, you're getting paid back in full, with interest, as soon as possible. And I'm going to ensure this never happens again. I've already earned you millions of dollars, and I'll continue doing so. I just chose the wrong method of laundering the cash. Laundering money isn't my forte: making money is."

He listened carefully, saying nothing. The guards bristled, hands on their guns, trigger fingers ready. They glanced out windows, then stared at me. The chef in the kitchen kept himself occupied with busywork. The waiter lingered nearby, waiting to take our orders immediately, but not daring to look anyone in the eye. This was the moment, I realized. I had no four million bucks to give him right now. That's probably what he expected, I would take out my phone and show him an account with four million of my own money in it. Wire-transfer it right then and there, and then go back to work. Again, I misjudged the situation due to my lack of experience, and now they would take me to an abandoned warehouse, a whole lot less inviting than this empty restaurant, and torture me for two days until I died of shock and blood loss. Idly, I wondered what the first method of torture would be. Then I wondered about the last.

I waited for El Jefe's response.

"Here's what we'll do," he said finally, slowly, spreading his hands on the table, showing his palms. "You will lay low for a while. A year. Just focus on the gambling; and when the time is right, we will reconnect. Make no mistake, I do expect you to make that money back for me."

"Yes, of course, absolutely. You will get it back, sir, every dollar and then a lot more where that came from. You have my word."

The lobster arrived, and El Jefe was a perfect gentleman. He smiled and said "*Buen provecho.*" There were a dozen lobsters between him and his *sicarios*, homemade flour tortillas prepared by a little Mexican lady in the back, rice, beans, fresh salsa, and lime wedges. Pacifico beers for everyone. The lobster was deep-fried to perfection, and on any other day I'd have eaten six of them myself. But not today.

I barely ate. I kept slugging quadruple-shot margs and wondering if this was all a ruse. Fatten up the pig and then hang him on a hook and bleed him dry. I knew there were extreme psychological torture methods the cartel employed. But in between bites of juicy buttery lobster, El Jefe kept saying "It's okay. You'll take a year off. Then I'm going to put you to work, and you will make all that money back and more."

I must have said "*Muchas gracias, Señor,*" a dozen times. I called him "*Viejon,*" which meant Boss of Bosses. I gave every indication possible that I would make him more money than ever before. Just let me do it in the way I was used to. At the end of the meal, he smiled, shook my hand, and said "You may go."

CHAPTER 7

My marching orders couldn't have been any clearer: lay low. There was simply no other option. In good faith, I'd brought along a copy of my driver's license to give to El Jefe during our meeting. I told him about my new family, my girlfriend and her two kids, and how this was the most recent address and he could verify it. Something about the way he received the copy told me he already had. Regardless, that meeting gave me a great deal of confidence moving forward. Where before I'd felt I was surely going to get whacked, now it was clear to me that I'd earned the Boss's respect, even if I'd just lost four million dollars of his money. At the end of the day, this was just a drop in the bucket for him, and I knew he saw something in me that could net far more than this. So, I was in the clear.

In the weeks after I got back to the States and started focusing on my gambling business, another gavel fell: this time, my mentors, Leo and Bo, were going down. Twenty FBI agents had surrounded their offices and arrested them. They were brought in on federal charges, their asses hauled back to America to face the music. I kept waiting for a knock at the door. Even El Jefe texted me, asking if this meant I was about to go to prison. I thought hard on what ties I had to Macho Sports . . . but I had none. I'd stopped working directly for them over a year ago.

As the days turned into weeks, my fear again transmuted into confidence. I'd gone to El Jefe thinking I was going to be tortured and killed, and I'd been given what . . . a promotion? My old bosses had been busted on federal international indictments, and I was still making cash from their business with the safety net of my own bookmaking, which started directly from them? I started feeling like I was untouchable. But then I got some news. Some of my colleagues, who had been released on bail with monitors attached to their ankles, were telling me to be careful. "When the feds were showing my lawyers and me their evidence, some of those photos had you in them. Be careful, O, is all I'm saying."

This did spook me, but nothing came of it. I kept flying down to Costa Rica, expanding and tightening up my gambling business, always half-expecting to be stopped at the airport and arrested, but nothing happened. Again, the fear subsided. What helped as well was the fact that Cipriani had jack shit to show the feds. I'd heard through the grapevine that he'd gone to the FBI in Philadelphia telling them about the money-laundering operation, naming me personally. They basically said "Who's this fucking idiot?" He had nothing to show for it, so they blew him off. When the Macho Sports bust went down and dozens of my old colleagues were being prosecuted on gambling racketeering indictments, all those old customers of Macho had nowhere else to go. I was able to get the customer list from Leo because I'd just spent two weeks canvassing Los Angeles to find him the best RICO attorney in the city. I got him a famous bookmaking lawyer who had represented members of the Gambino crime family, along with the real-life Henry Hill from the movie *Goodfellas*. Leo returned the favor by giving me a few dozen of his best agents who hadn't been indicted, along with his VIP customers who now needed a website to place bets with. My operation became one of the biggest sports books around, virtually overnight. I recruited a few sub-bookies who'd been brought to me by old Macho associates, offering the same rates as they had been getting with Macho. A turnkey sports book that had been operating for twenty years was handed to me on a silver platter. I even went and visited Leo while he was under house arrest, asking him about all the ins and outs of his business model.

"What do I do about these customers?" I'd ask. "And these VIP agents, how do you treat them?"

Leo's number one response was "Make Vegas your best friend, and you'll be just fine."

I started wining and dining my new VIPs O-Dog style. Every agent in the business wanted to bring their customers to me after a weekend in Vegas. Like the brothers used to do, I'd fly the VIPs first class to Vegas, put them up in a penthouse suite at the Aria, have ten of the hottest strippers from Spearmint Rhino and Sapphire show up at the Encore Beach Club where I'd have a group of NFL players and pro UFC fighters shelling out $500 an hour on the girls. In addition, I ramped up the libertine atmosphere by tossing disco biscuits into the strippers' and VIPs' mouths along with some GHB to wash it all down, and they knew they were in for the best twenty-four hours of their lives. Frequently the agents would stagger up to me by the end of the weekend and embrace me as if I were their long-lost brother from before the war. There was one thing they all knew: their money was safe with me.

As my gambling business started booming, I still ran little errands for El Jefe here and there. Drop off a few hundred grand in this stash house in Downey, California, or run this few hundred grand up north.

I wasn't aware at the time, but Cipriani was getting closer to cutting a deal with the Feds. He was doing anything he could to bring me down in exchange for legal immunity. He called me sometimes.

"Hey, man, I want to make good on that money. What do we got to do?" But I didn't want to even speak with him. Something felt off. Instead, I hired that old private investigator I'd used in the past to help me track people down and collect money for the sports book.

At a café sitting across from me, after having plied himself with a huge double portion of huevos rancheros, Danno said confidently "I know a guy. They call him 'Animal.'"

This was a great start.

"All right," I said. "I'm listening."

Danno scooped the last smears of beans up with a wet floppy tortilla and inhaled it, chewing loudly. He spoke as he chewed. "Big guy. Real scary-looking."

"Guess that's why they call him Animal."

Danno nodded. "He's a good collector. Decent rates. Wanna use him?"

Sure, why not. What's the worst that could happen? Put a little fear of God the Almighty into Cipriani, and maybe he'd finally start making payments and stop these awkward exchanges over the phone. Animal and some other guys started showing up at Cipriani's condo. They would call his phone with threats. Animal left a letter in Portuguese to Cipriani's wife, saying that her husband had really fucked up with the wrong people, which meant she was in trouble too. These were scare tactics, there was no intention to actually cause anybody physical harm. And they did work, to a degree, scaring the living shit out of Cipriani. But unbeknownst to me, these formed the catalyst of his increasingly habitual return to the FBI.

"Look, man, I got them on videotape outside of my house!" he said. He shared the threatening phone calls, the letter. And he wouldn't pay up a single dime. The bastard even went so far as to call up my customers and tell them I was about to be taken down by the FBI, and do you happen to know anything they could use against him? Like an evil ex, he was playing some real fucking mind games, and it was accomplishing nothing more than pissing me off. I decided the best course of action was to just ignore him and work on getting the several million back in my own way.

After about a year of laying low, I got ahold of a contact I'd made, Greg Huber, who was one of the biggest cocaine kingpins in Sydney, Australia. The Australian lawyer who had been trying to get El Jefe's $700k back, minus his cut, of course, had been introduced to me by Huber. I had to break down to Huber how exactly I'd lost the money, and he said "Man, any time you want to work the proper way, I can make sure this operation is done a lot cleaner and you'll never have to worry about washing all that money, it'll just get sent to you in the States within a couple weeks." I never forgot this, as he was one of the top gangsters in Kings Cross, the major party scene of Sydney. If anyone knew how to do it, it was him.

Huber invited me to Fiji to discuss business with his friend Alex Patini, who owned a private island called Vatulele reserved exclusively for his friends and family. When I asked why he didn't want to meet in Australia, he said "You're hotter than a two-dollar pistol right now, mate." That was fine by me. I let El Jefe know that I thought it was time to get back into the game, and I was on my way to discuss business with my mates down under. I had essentially inherited Macho Sports scot-free, and I was facing no legal ramifications from that or from the Australia bust. El Jefe gave me his blessing.

Greg and I showed up on the private five-star island to a royal welcome from the locals. Patini spared no expense, showing us to our own private villas mere feet from the majestic aqua-blue water and white-sand beach. Joining us were my girl, her sister, and Greg's wife. While the girls went off to the local watering hole for cocktails, we sat in the courtyard of Greg's massive estate to talk business.

On the table was Kokoda, a local cuisine, as well as all types of fresh sushi, mud crabs, golden lobster, and bottles of white wine and champagne on ice.

Before I got there, El Jefe had impressed upon me the need to start a whole new operation from the ground up. No ties to the previous contacts. He was a firm believer in not having any attention bounce back on his network. He had middlemen upon middlemen upon middlemen, a hundred degrees of separation, which was what had enabled him to build his empire below the radar for so long.

As I was twirling a glass of the wine, Patini looked at me and said "Do you have any ideas, Owen?"

I held my wine glass up to the sun. "I'll break down the cocaine and ship it in bottles of white wine. We'll use dark-glass bottles so it'll look like any other liquid. Once the shipment is received in Australia, a chemist will go about breaking down the liquid cocaine back into powder form, a team will press it into bricks, and we're good to sell to our buyers in Australia."

They thought the idea was fucking novel. It was a go.

Within weeks, Huber called me up excitedly saying he'd found my chemist. He had a guy who would clear the shipments of cocaine wine on the Australian side; all we needed now was to ensure it left America from a winery without any hang-ups. I called El Jefe saying I needed ten kilos brought to the office of my new construction and real estate development company, which I'd founded with a guy named Charlie D'Agostino. Our company had been successfully doing the buildouts for custom-made homes in the South Bay, mostly Redondo and Hermosa Beach, and occasionally in Hollywood and Beverly Hills. It was a legitimate business, the perfect front. Now not only was I selling coke to the crème de la crème of the Hollywood elite, I was also building their homes.

At this point, between the massive success of both my gambling business and my legitimate real estate company, I really didn't need to be dealing cocaine. But I was on the line for millions to El Jefe, and I certainly owed him some favors for electing not to fucking whack me. I told him "I'll have your money back within a month."

"There's no fucking way," he said.

"I got the guy and the method. I'm going to make it happen."

My plan was to get El Jefe's money back with interest, then leave the drug business behind forever and focus on my burgeoning real estate and gambling businesses only. That was the plan, anyway.

But sometimes life doesn't give a fuck about your plans.

CHAPTER 8

My real estate business partner Charlie and I were in his warehouse. In front of us, ten kilos of cocaine sat on a shop table. We had two cases of 95 percent Everclear alcohol and two cases of dark-tinted white Napa wine bottles. We also had corks, wax, and a do-it-yourself corking machine. A bathtub sat beside the table. I told Charlie I was going to start dumping out all the wine, and since he was an alcoholic, he'd better get something to pour it in if he wanted it. He ran and grabbed a couple of 5-gallon water dispensers.

"Owen," Charlie said, examining the scene. "What the *fuck* are we doing here?"

I grabbed a bottle of Everclear, opened it, and took a little pull. I instantly spit it out. "The fuck!"

"Yeah, dude. It's pure booze. You want brain damage, or what?"

"No, got enough of that already. Charlie, start grabbing those kilos and bring them over to the tub."

"Why?"

"Just do it, man. I'll show you."

Charlie dutifully carried over kilos of cocaine. I gave him a box cutter and told him to dump the cocaine into the tub while I grabbed the rest of the kilos. He stared at me with an expression that said "You're fucking insane." Reminded me of all those UGG conversations I'd had in the past. *Is Owen off his rocker? Why does he keep buying us all these UGGs!* No. There was a method to my madness.

"This is exactly what the chemist told me to do. Go ahead, dump that shit. Take a few bumps if you want."

I had a few myself. Once all the cocaine had been dumped into the tub, we went about topping it off with Everclear, a couple of mad scientists leaned over stirring the concoction with metal spoons and bugged out eyes. The liquid became a thick white milky substance; but after pouring in more booze, it started shifting to clear, just like white wine. We used glass Pyrex measuring cups to scoop out the liquid cocaine and poured it in the wine bottles via metal funnels. Once every last drop was in bottles, we corked them and melted wax over the tops. We placed one bottle of the liquid cocaine in with a case of legitimate wine and sent it abroad. Within ten days, my chemist contact in Sydney got back to me. "It worked," he said. He was able to bake the liquid back into its pure form, getting rid of the alcohol entirely by cooking it off.

It was around Christmas time, which according to El Jefe was the best time of the year for smuggling because gifts were coming in en masse from all over the world. So I got ahold of El Jefe and said "Boss, they're ready. It's Feliz Navidad." He had fifteen more kilos dropped off at my offices, and the two mad scientists were at it again, pouring liquid coke into wine bottles, corking and waxing the tops, then rubbing clear any trace of cocaine residue with rubbing alcohol. We packaged and shipped them as a Holiday sample from Napa Valley via DHL to Australia, clearing customs with our guy in Sydney who was taking a 50 percent cut. I brought this to the Boss's attention. "Isn't that a bit steep?"

He said "Who cares? We're quadrupling our money now. We can bring in as much as we want and no longer have to worry about laundering the money." And he was right. The 50 percent take on the customs guy's end paled in comparison to the absolute fuckery it would be for me to launder the sheer amount of money we were now bringing in. The process was as easy as a quick sale, then Huber would have our cut wired to a bank in Dubai for us, and from there to Mexico City. There was no need for Cipriani. No more gold bullion. No more counting cash on a janky machine. No more fake IDs.

Because we were using 95 percent alcohol to mix with the cocaine, it meant our yield would be 95 percent for each kilo. So instead of 1000 grams per kilo, we had 950, but that didn't matter, because we had the purest cocaine in the world. We could afford to lose fifty grams per kilo. Pretty soon, Charlie and I had moved out of the warehouse and were mixing our cocaine concoctions in the bathtubs of the buildouts at various job sites we had. My deal with him was he'd make a thousand bucks per kilo sold, and he was all too happy to oblige.

But all good things must come to an end, especially when money is involved. After a few weeks, our chemist started growing overconfident. He wanted to charge a premium, and the deal wasn't making sense anymore. El Jefe asked if I could come up with another idea.

The Dully brothers were a few friends from USC who worked for their family's import-export business, which shipped luxury European chocolates all over the world. I saw an opportunity there. I attended a wedding I knew they were going to and got them good and drunk. Late into the evening at the bar, I said quietly to them "Listen, I may have a business opportunity for you guys. How would you like to make $50k cash every month?"

They were drunk, but not so plastered that the cash figure went over their heads. "Fuck, that sounds good. What would we have to do?"

I explained that all I needed was the product from their expired chocolate. They had a 20,000-square-foot warehouse full of chocolate and candy products from Europe; I was sure a decent portion routinely went bad.

"Sure," they said, intrigued. "That's more than possible."

I bought us another round. "When we're sober, let's all go grab some coffee and I'll explain further."

Within days, we were at a coffee shop and I was going through the plan. I explained that all I needed was their boxes and expired chocolate, and I'd show them how to package the coke for shipping. My boss had routes going from Chicago to Canada, but one of his trucks had recently been stopped with two hundred raw kilos, all confiscated. The brothers agreed to let us do a test run; so after hours, as the sun was setting, I met them at the loading dock of their warehouse. A car came and parked, and a small Mexican man got out and opened the trunk. He lifted the rug off the trunk, then pressed a hidden button on the wall, and a hydraulic lift opened a hidden compartment with fifty kilos of coke. One of the brothers muttered "Holy shit."

Together we packaged the kilos in with the chocolates. We started by vacuum-sealing the coke so no scent could be detected. Then we took all the chocolate out of boxes and covered the bottoms of the boxes with the kilos, four to a box. After thirteen boxes, we placed them in the center of a pallet, packed another twenty boxes of legitimate product around it, and wrapped the pallet in Saran wrap. I had them delivered via DHL truck to Toronto.

El Jefe texted me in a panic. "We got the truck but can't find the cocaine. All we see are chocolates. Holy shit, where is the coke?" I told them to break down the center boxes completely—and, sure enough, there were all the kilos I'd hidden at the very bottoms of the boxes with chocolate bars. El Jefe was amazed.

"I'll take $1,000 off your tab for every kilo you're able to send in this way, and $500 to the Dully brothers."

It was a no-brainer. El Jefe was already shipping two hundred kilos a week. That meant $200k per week worked off my debt. I also persuaded him to start shipping the chocolates to Australia as samples. Pretty soon, the entire operation was back up and running. Charlie was making his thousand bucks a key, the Dully brothers were making $50k a month, I was working off $200k a week via the Canadian route, and now we were sending hundreds of thousands in kilos a week to the hottest market of Australia. They started calling me the California Kid.

I'd intended to pay off El Jefe within one month, but because of the time it took on Greg Huber's end to clean and wire the money to us, it ended up taking three months. I asked whether there was any way to speed up the process. He texted me on the Phantom Secure one day, saying he'd been on his yacht hosting a party, and two American guys had nonchalantly said they were in the money-cleaning business. He said "Maybe we should see what they're capable of. It takes my Pakistani guys three weeks to get your money to you. These two guys said they could do it in a week. They're in the San Diego area. Maybe you all can meet over a round of golf."

I told him sure. What did I have to lose?

"His name is Al Wilson," Greg had told me.

I was walking into the golf course, one of the most prestigious country clubs in San Diego. Greg said to me a week before, "Why don't we try these guys with some small money and see what they can do?" He gave them ten grand from Australia to get back to the

States in cash.

As I entered the lobby, a guy in a tropical shirt walked over to me. "Owen?" he said.

I was a little put off. He must have noticed my surprise, because he said, "Greg told me what you look like. 'Athletic build, faux-hawk, walks with swagger.'" He gave me a crooked smile. "Man, where are my manners." He extended his hand. "Al Wilson."

I shook it. "Right. Owen."

Another smile. "Come on, man, let's meet the guys and grab some drinks."

Al led me to the bar where two other men were waiting for us. He introduced one of them as George, a guy who was in the Swiss banking business, who lives in Switzerland and handles all the major illicit accounts and transactions from there. The third guy was in the boating business and physically transported large sums of money via his yacht. It felt like we were in a group therapy session of drug dealers and money launderers. "I'm Bob. I transport cocaine across international borders." "Oh, swell! I'm Kyle. I launder money for the cartel." And so on. It certainly was one of the strangest first meetings I'd ever had. Al ordered a round of margaritas and shots of Don Julio.

"Oh, shit," he said. Reaching into his back pocket, he pulled out a fat envelope and handed it to me. "Your nine Gs. Minus my 10 percent cut, of course."

I ran my thumb through the bills. I didn't even need to count it to know it was correct. "Thanks, Al. You managed that in a week?"

He shrugged. "As I told your pal Huber, we're not amateurs. And this is just a taste." He put his hand on my shoulder. "Come on, get your drink. Let's play some golf."

We spent the morning playing golf, downing drinks, popping Vicodins. At one point, Al took out a Phantom Secure phone, texting on it. Then he put it away. He caught my eye. "You know what that is?"

I nodded. "I have one. Couldn't do my business without it."

Al nodded back. "Same."

If he had one of those, Greg was right; he was the real fucking deal. It set my anxiety at ease, so I continued to let them get me all liquored up. Finally, drunkenly, my vision blurry and my motor skills slightly deficient, I said "So, what's good, fellas? How can we start earning together? Break down exactly what you guys do, as I don't normally meet with strangers like this."

"We can launder money anywhere in the world, Owen," Al said, teeing up. His shoulders slumped, his front foot pointed too far to the left, his stance too open. *This guy isn't very good at golf,* I realized. He took a swing, nearly sliced it. I don't think he even noticed because he seemed proud of himself, watching the ball soar awkwardly somewhat in the direction of the hole. "What are you paying for that right now?" he asked coolly.

"Twenty-five percent."

My stomach growled. I'd had a lot of booze and hadn't eaten anything but a protein bar. It was soon to be a fight-or-flight scenario, involving the posh tiled bathroom back at the clubhouse. I hoped I wouldn't throw up on Al.

"We'd cut that figure right in half. Twelve and a half percent."

"I like the sound of that. What's your timeframe?"

"One week, across the board. No more. Possibly less."

"You're shitting me."

"No, sir."

"From Australia too?"

"Especially Australia, yes."

After the eighteenth hole, I was ready to be back at the clubhouse, where Al plied me with yet more liquor and hors d'oeuvres. After making a mess of the bathroom, I returned feeling refreshed and in need of more alcohol. I noticed Al and the other guys on their iPhones, making bets on a football game.

"Whoa, you bet on sports?"

"Fuck, yes," he said.

"I'm a bookie myself. Here, I'll get you set up with my site."

I created accounts for all three on BetODog and gave them 20 percent discounts on their first week of bets, on the house. They loved the look of it and started betting. I wanted to call Greg and tell him it was a go. I mean, not only were they going to get El Jefe and my money to us within a week instead of three, they were doing it at 12.5 percent. And I had them betting on my site? This was a win-win. Not only that, but they had Phantom Secure phones.

I was sold.

After the meeting, I texted Greg. He was ecstatic. We decided we'd use Al for the next chocolate shipment of a few million dollars to Australia. The shipment landed in Australia, and a week later, I had the money in my offshore account.

Al had pulled through.

CHAPTER 9

O ver time, El Jefe started taking me under his wing.

It was little things, at first. Small indications of respect and camaraderie. Calls from him at 4:00 in the morning when his men couldn't find the packages of cocaine I'd so skillfully hidden in the shipment. I would answer on the first ring, always, and calmly explain where they were: "Have your men go down to crate six. You'll find twelve boxes of chocolates in there; the coke's in the very back left and right corner, at the bottom. You'll see the scorpion stamp."

"Ah, yes, yes. They say they found it. And the Rolex-stamped ones?"

"Box seven. Same deal, in the back corners at the very bottom."

The scorpion-stamped kilos had come from Colombia, the Rolex ones from Peru.

"Thank you, Owen," he'd say. And I could hear the genuine gratitude in his voice. He knew, day or night, he could call me and I would pick up on the first ring. It was our unspoken agreement. Didn't matter if I was coked out of my mind on a bender with a group of VIPs or about to hop on a flight halfway around the world and needed to close some pressing business before I went dark. If El Jefe called, I picked up the phone.

I learned little intricacies about his personality. He was well educated and incredibly smart. His English was impeccable.

He was also phenomenal at numbers. He would text me figures on the encrypted phone: "We had three hundred kilos go out, twenty were on this truck." He would subtract all the costs from shipping and the people he had working for us and give me a number that was always correct down to the decimal point. Then he would tell me my cut. Sometimes I would call him and say "Why am I paying that six hundred on the courier fee? I thought that was you." He would tell me to look at line item two, and, sure enough, it showed the proper deduction, and the math was sound. He double- and triple-checked everything. He had dozens of operations going on at once, thousands of people working under him. He kept it all in line with mathematical precision.

El Jefe never did drugs, and he barely drank. Sometimes he would have a glass of wine with dinner when we'd go out to the five-star resort in Pedregal. There would be a coterie of gorgeous women I brought in from Vegas snorting blow and getting shitfaced, and he'd sit there calmly eating food and sipping champagne, happy as a clam as he listened to them talk and laugh.

Because he was . . . well, a drug kingpin, and wanted not only in Mexico but by the DEA in the U.S., El Jefe didn't have the same freedoms enjoyed by most people. He couldn't just tag along with me on a Vegas trip, so I brought Vegas to him. I brought star NFL players, showgirls, models, you name it, and he would treat them like they were the only people on Earth. If there was a girl he particularly liked, he would fly her back a week later on a private plane for a set of veneers or a boob job. He'd take me aside: "Hey, Owen, that girl, Nadia? Does she need new breasts, or a Brazilian butt lift?" It was his thing, and he was very giving in that regard. He became known for these grand gestures.

But there was also a ruthless side to him.

Once I overheard a conversation he was having on the phone. A guy from Guatemala had sent him a hundred kilos of bunk coke. A hundred kilos at ten grand apiece, that was a million bucks El Jefe was now out. The guy who'd brokered the deal was a Mexican who worked for him. El Jefe stood stock still a few feet from me, speaking calmly into the phone: "Listen, if the man who did this deal in Guatemala is not dead within one week, it will be you. Do I make myself clear?"

El Jefe made no mention of it when he got off the call. He sat down calmly, and we proceeded to talk about the latest Super Bowl. But when I saw him next, he said, nonchalantly, "That guy in Guatemala who ripped me off? He was taken care of."

I don't know why he told me this. Was it a warning, or was it his way of indicating he thought of me differently than these other guys? It left an indelible impression on me, for obvious reasons. This Guatemalan had deceived El Jefe out of a million dollars, and he was dead within a week. Although I hadn't deceived El Jefe, I'd lost nearly *four million dollars* of his money, and I was not only allowed to live the entire year it took before I could make it back, but he also now counted me among his closest associates in America.

Maybe he even counted me as a friend.

Because business was going so well, El Jefe had me send my boy Tank out to New Jersey to set up an East Coast operation. Tank was half black and Italian. He was given his nickname as a kid because he was built like a tank. He was one of the original gangsters of one of the oldest Crip gangs in Los Angeles, the Avalon Crips, which was in the heart of the city. He'd started as my muscle and bodyguard but became so well trusted, I made him my second in command of the ODog operation.

At this point, I was all caught up on paying El Jefe back, and he started fronting me fifty kilos at a time at the same cost he was paying in Mexico, which made my profit around thirty grand a kilo. He set Tank up with a nice four-bedroom house in a gated suburban community just ten miles from the Dully brothers' New Jersey chocolate warehouse, and we used several vehicles provided by El Jefe that had hidden hydraulic compartments for stashing cocaine, as well as the trucks from the chocolate warehouse.

Our operation was so smooth, we now had bigwigs in the marijuana business tapping us for our transportation routes. Guys in California who grew Sour Diesel and Purple Kush, which went for a hell of a lot more over on the East Coast, now started paying me $500 a pound to move their 200-pound shipments across the country alongside our own. Same went for the China white heroin Tank had a market for in the tri-state area; he would stash the heroin in the cars' secret compartments, set out around town, and come back with a few hundred grand in cash. It was free money. I even had a bathtub installed at his house that was geared to a hydraulic system, which would raise the tub, revealing a compartment where you could stash a million dollars cash or twenty kilos of cocaine.

We started moving to the water too. I'd had one of my workers, Pauly, practicing sailing for the past year. He met me in Puerto Nuevo, Mexico, the same place where El Jefe and I had had our fateful meeting the year before. El Jefe was using a fifty-five-foot catamaran I'd repossessed from a gambling customer of mine for not paying his debts. El Jefe retrofitted it with a secret hydraulic compartment storing a hundred kilos of cocaine, and it was my job to get it to San Diego without any trouble. I took my girlfriend Stephanie with me, and the three of us went onto the boat with one of El Jefe's men, who showed us the proper buttons to hit to open the secret compartment once the boat was safe and sound in a harbor in Newport Beach. When all was said and done, El Jefe's contact handed us the keys, I gave them to Pauly and sent him on his way, and Stephanie and I had lobster at the same restaurant where I'd once thought I was having my last meal.

She was shaking.

"Are you nervous?" I asked her.

"Y-yes," she stammered. She kept drinking margaritas.

I put my hand over hers. "Don't be nervous, babe. These are my people. We're perfectly safe."

Stephanie smiled, weakly at first, but she saw the sincerity in my eyes. She held up her glass. "To Owen Hanson," she said. We clinked glasses, and later that night we had sex for hours, due in no small part to the bag of ecstasy and the mountain of blow on the coffee table of my penthouse suite. When we'd finished, I glanced around the massive bedroom, realizing how far I'd come since those days back at USC when I'd stored drugs in my sock drawer, and, before that, rolling around in sheets full of sand at my dad's house, eating meals off paper plates on my lap in the small living room.

I had paid El Jefe back and then some. I was free to leave now, to chart my own course, a legitimate course that would one day see me rise through the ranks of business and finance like so many of my peers who had graduated from USC. I'd promised myself I would be done with the drug business once I was square with El Jefe. The truth was, that was a lie I told myself to get through my day-to-day, to justify my actions moving forward. I'd always known I wouldn't stop. I liked the drug business . . . no, I *loved* it. And I was fucking good at it, so why would I stop now?

The truth was, I felt like a king.

CHAPTER 10

"This guy Cipriani keeps calling me again," my dad said.

We were sitting at a restaurant in Redondo Beach on a Saturday afternoon, waves lapping at the shore. Surfers were far out in the blue, carving, falling, laughing. A group of kids rushed past, boogie boards under their little arms. A couple of cold beers sat in front of us. I brought mine to my lips, then shook my head and set it down. "What's he saying?" I asked, annoyed.

My dad shrugged. "All this crazy stuff. 'Your son is going down. He's involved in money laundering. You need to tell him to back off.'"

"And what did you say?"

"Just what you told me. This isn't gambling money. It goes a lot higher than that and that's all I know. I said 'Listen, I think you must realize it's not even my son's money. I'm sure soon enough you'll find out who it belongs to.'" My dad looked at me seriously. "Owen, what's he mean, 'back off'? What are you doing?"

"Nothing, Pops," I lied, taking a sip of beer. I knew exactly what Cipriani had meant.

For a while, Cipriani had been trying to entrap me somehow, get me admitting on the phone what we had done together in Australia and to agree that I was ready to launder some more money. He was downright insistent. "Hey, man, we gotta get that 2.5 mil back. When do you want to do the next round? We can go down to Costa Rica." I just placated him, said don't worry about it, we'll figure it out in time. Just in the meanwhile drop a few thousand in this account when you can, a few thousand in this one. Some good-faith deposits. He never did. What he did instead was pay some guy at T-Mobile a hundred bucks to access my contacts list and then change the password on me. This is how he was able to start hitting up all my contacts. I eventually went into a T-Mobile to figure out what had happened, and the customer service guy told me this was a common thing, and we just needed to change the password back. When I saw what the password had been changed to, I knew it was Cipriani. The password was: fuckyou. He started spoofing his numbers to the FBI office out of L.A. and calling me from it. I would call the number back and reach the FBI and get freaked the fuck out. He would also call me from a spoof number using a female voice. He was playing games with me.

That's when I started ramping up the threats with the letters to his wife, and I even hired my PI Danno Hanks to make a trip to Pennsylvania. I told him if he could bring me Cipriani's mother's tombstone as collateral I'd pay him an extra five grand. But when he showed up he realized the tombstone was six feet tall and weighed over five hundred pounds, so he resorted to our Plan B: splashing red paint on the gravestone was Danno's idea, to indicate blood. When Danno left the cemetery, he called me. "I did the paint, there's just one problem. It isn't going to wash off."

"What do you mean it's not going to wash off?"

"It's oil-based, not water-based."

"Goddammit, Danno. I didn't want the paint on there forever. Whatever, just do the photo and send it to me."

But he didn't send it to me, he sent it straight to Cipriani after cropping a Halloween photo of me in a Lucha Libre mask holding a shovel. Danno also included a list of all Cipriani's family members' addresses, phone numbers, and license plates. It was a threat, clearly. "Pay me my fucking money, bitch. Or you'll end up right here in the ground at your parents' plot." It cost me a hundred bucks. It was foolish, for sure, but I had no intention of harming the guy, I just wanted him to pay up.

But this is not what put the fear of God into Cipriani. At some point through all this, El Jefe had a video sent to him.

In the video, three men were tied up. There was a chainsaw, the men whimpering, crying, praying to God. A Mexican man in a mask was revving the chainsaw, then methodically cutting off their heads while they were still alive. When he'd finished, he looked into the camera and said, in Spanish, "This is what we do to people who steal from us. Don't think you're not going to pay us back our money."

This must have sent Cipriani into overdrive, because soon after that El Jefe told me to have no further contact with him and to lie low, as the feds were tailing me. This had been a while back, and I'd not heard from Cipriani in many months. So why was he calling my dad again now?

"Are you in any kind of trouble?" my dad asked. "Is there anything I should worry about?"

"No, Pops," I assured him. "Everything is fine. Let's enjoy our beers."

It all started with my real estate business partner, Charlie.

I was in Mexico playing a golf tournament with a bookie friend of mine, Matt Bowyer. We routinely bet $50,000 a week on these tournaments, and we were enjoying some cold margaritas on the tenth hole when I got a call from Charlie, who was supposed to go pick up a hundred grand from El Jefe's runner. He said he was going to drop off a heater with Tank at one of the real estate job sites, to speed up the gluing process on some hardwood floors, and he'd let me know when he'd made it back to his house in Redondo with the money.

This was fine. I played golf. Drank. Snorted some bumps of cocaine. When the tournament was over, I headed back to my suite at the Four Seasons and had dinner. I called Charlie, as it was getting late and he should have gotten back hours ago. No answer. I kept calling. No answer. I tried Tank as well . . . no answer.

What the fuck?

I called obsessively, the same creeping feeling of my associate Sean going dark on me in Australia. Something had happened, I knew. Finally at two in the morning I got through to Charlie.

"What the fuck happened?" were the first words out of my mouth.

Charlie's voice was shaking. "O, the DEA task force was following me. They had helicopters in the air above my fucking house. They came in and took the money, went in the safe and took all your gold bullion and your cash. They confiscated everything! Took me to the police department, but I didn't say shit."

"Nothing at all?"

"No, man!"

"Why did they release you?"

"I have no idea! They gave me no charges. No explanation."

I sighed. That was a million dollars in bullion they had taken. What the hell was going on? I told Charlie to chill and lie low and called Tank. Same story. The DEA had followed him to his house and ripped apart the floor heater Charlie had given him, thinking there was cocaine inside it. Luckily he had no coke in the house, but he had an entire marijuana grow operation. They took all his plants and the seven grand he had on him. They didn't arrest him either.

There was no way I was going back to the States. They were rounding up all my employees but not arresting them? That meant there was only one person they were after: me. I had Danno Hanks drive by my house and some of my construction sites. He reported that there were telephone company vans parked out in several locations, and when he ran the plates, they came back as FBI.

This was not good.

———————————

I laid low in Mexico for a week, and the situation went from bad to worse.

Frantic calls from Charlie telling me our accounts at Wells Fargo and Chase were under scrutiny. The banks kept asking him about the large offshore wires coming in, which were from El Jefe, and all he said was they were from investors in our real estate business. Frank, the owner of the private vault where I kept a lot of my bullion and cash, had called me saying the FBI had come by asking about me. "You need to get in here and get everything out," he told me.

Charlie said "You need to get back here, O. Everything is going sideways."

I went back to the States.

———————————

Al Wilson had been laundering batches of a quarter million dollars for us with no issues whatsoever. I was doing a buildout on a 3,000-square-foot Italian restaurant in Los Angeles, with plans for another one in Cabo San Lucas, around 10 miles away from El Jefe's estate in Pedregal. All the laundered money from Wilson was getting sent to my contractors on the build.

Wilson and I had been meeting weekly over drinks at five-star hotels in San Diego to discuss business. This time around, the vibe was different. Something had shifted, in me, in business, in him.

We sat at the bar, me high as fuck on cocaine and a bit drunk, a morning routine that had started ever since I got that call from Charlie the week before saying the DEA had raided his house. I'd been in the States for several days and still had not been taken down. We'd been talking about some of the recent drops. This guy at the far end of the bar kept looking at us—a brute of a man, tattoos criss-crossing his muscled arms. He stuck out like a sore thumb.

I watched Al carefully. "You know, if you're with the feds, my people in Mexico are not just going to kill me, they're going to kill you too."

Al seemed completely stunned. I'd given him something with this comment. There was a revelation in his eyes. He quickly blinked it away. "I'm not with the feds," he said.

I pointed down the bar. "Who is that guy? He's been staring at us this whole fucking time, and he's not with me."

Al shrugged. "No idea, man. Look, you okay? Maybe you ought to lay off all that coke. It's making you, like, paranoid."

Me, paranoid? Sure. It wasn't that he took my girl and me out to dinner and paid a 100 percent tip on the bill. *Nobody* does that. Not even the most generous super-rich clients I work with. Not even El Jefe, who is more generous than them all. It was an amateur move, weird, out of place. Just like him plying my girl for information about my cartel connections while I was in the bathroom. I didn't like any of it. Not one bit.

When we left the bar, Al pulled me aside. "Look, man, sorry I couldn't say this earlier, but that guy *is* with me. He's my security for meetings."

"Why the hell would you need security at a five-star restaurant when you're just talking to me?"

"It's a precaution. That's all."

"Why didn't you mention it at the bar, then? Why are you telling me now?"

"I don't know who's listening at that bar. I don't know who those guys are, sitting around me, they could be anyone." He scoffed. "I can't mention that sort of thing in public."

But it didn't add up. I studied him a moment. "Hey, let me get a picture of your ID. I just want to run your information."

Al paused, confused. "Uh, no, I don't think so."

"Come on, just let me get your ID."

Al said nothing.

"Listen, everyone I do business with, I get a picture of their ID. It's common procedure and I just haven't done it yet. It's really not a big deal."

But Al wouldn't do it.

I left that meeting sour and more paranoid. Didn't help that a few days later, he asked for five kilos—or "birds," as we called it. He said he was into his own operation now, sending coke to Australia, and he wondered if he could buy it off me for the price I charged in L.A., around $30k a bird. I persuaded him to take another five of mine along his route to sell for me, and I'd just pay for his transportation costs and fees to clear customs.

A week later, one of Al's people was meeting with Tank for a money pickup. Fifty thousand dollars. Tank called me from the bathroom. "Yo, are you sure this is your guy? He's in a fucking Hawaiian T-shirt. Who wears a Hawaiian T-shirt in New York City?"

In between bumps of coke, I told Tank it was legit, to calm down and just give him the money. But after the meeting, Tank said the guy asked him point-blank: "This money is for your boss, right?"

"I don't know what you're talking about," Tank said. "I don't have a boss."

"Your boss, O-Dog, right?"

Tank just gave him the money, saying he had no idea what he was talking about. But it didn't sit right with him. With me either. Tank said he thought the guy was an undercover agent. Maybe he was.

There were other red flags too.

I wanted to check up on Tank's operation on the East Coast, so I flew over there for a few days to make sure everything was good. Wilson told me I should stop into Miami on the way back home to check out his warehouse. Wilson and his business partner picked me up by the Fontainebleau Hotel in a cigarette boat. They fed me Don Julio shots, driving at forty knots and slicing through the surf. When we finally arrived at their 10,000-square-foot warehouse, I was half drunk. We were greeted by the tatted guy from the bar. "I've seen him before," I said drunkenly. "He was with you in San Diego."

"Yeah, he works for me," Al said nonchalantly.

The tatted guy got us into a truck and took us a couple blocks to the warehouse. When we got out, Al had me leave all my cell phones in the vehicle. "We don't allow any phones or encrypted devices in the garage," he said. "We can't risk any photos being taken of this stuff."

I was intrigued.

Inside, I understood why. There were dozens of brand-new cars and trucks, all with hidden compartments for cash and cocaine. They even had a tool-shop compressor with a panel that popped off, where you could store a million dollars cash. They had a Chevy Silverado where if you pressed the brake pedal and then hit the window switch up and down, secret compartments would come out. These were the most sophisticated stash spots I'd ever seen.

We had yet more drinks in a back room, and at this point I was positively shitfaced. They wanted to start their own operation in Australia in a big way. Clearly, they had the means and the sophisticated equipment to make it happen. They were asking me pointed questions: "Do you think if we send enough product down there, you can move it? In the past, who were you working with to move your product?" I was cocky. All I said was they didn't need to know the specifics; I could handle it. I worked with the cartel, and we knew what we were doing. In my drunken stupor, I couldn't help but posture around these guys. Yes, I had an Uncle Louie down there who could move whatever they wanted; he worked for an international fucking drug syndicate. I mentioned the Assyrian Kings, Hell's Angels, the Banditos, the Nomads. I said I had the best contacts out there; one of them ran the whole coke operation of King's Cross. I closed it by saying "If you hand over the birds, I'll have a million dollars cash waiting for you at one of our stash houses."

"And what if we want to sail the product. Do you have a boat to use?"

I gave a dismissive wave. "Yeah, don't worry about it. I got a fifty-five-foot catamaran that can store around a hundred birds."

"Do you have a captain to get it there?"

"Of course."

"Right on. Well, we have one too."

If I hadn't been so fucking drunk, maybe I would have picked up on this. If they have a captain already, why are they asking me if I've got one?

Later, back on the cigarette boat, I texted El Jefe about the warehouse. He said "Those are agents. No one in the business would ever show you the toys and secrets to their business." I could have thrown up. Around me, Wilson and his partner were having a ball of a time, drinking more booze and cracking jokes. They tried to give me more tequila, and I couldn't stomach it.

"What's the matter?" Wilson said.

"Nothing. I'm just tired."

The next several days passed in a haze of drug-and-booze-fueled paranoia.

With no sleep, I hopped on a plane from Miami back to L.A., where I sat next to Bradley Cooper. I was drifting in and out of sleep as people kept coming up to first class to pester him, waking me up. At one point, I muttered "God, how fucking annoying," and he laughed. I faded, fell back asleep, and woke up in a private car on the way to Mountain Gate, my country club, with Samuel L. Jackson and Justin Timberlake playing in front of my bookie friends and me. I was losing every single hole. I could barely stand upright.

My friend said "What's the matter with you, man?"

I snorted some coke. Took more G. "I'm fine," I said.

As we turned the corner on hole nine coming up to ten, I spotted Frank, the owner of the private vault I used, on the putting green. He called me over. I ambled up to him and he whispered in my ear: "Listen, they came back again, buddy. They're trying to subpoena my private security cameras. They're going to get them soon. Whatever you have, get it now and skip town. They're coming for you fast."

More cocaine. Nips of tequila. A couple Vicodin. A Purell bottle of GHB.

It was the next morning, and I could hardly focus on the freeway, weaving my Porsche in and out of traffic, speeding to my ex Desiree's subterranean garage, the world in front of me a terrifying blend of speed and light and fear. At the garage I chucked all my phones, aside from one Phantom Secure, into the car and locked it up. They'd tagged my car with a tracking device. Must have. I grabbed my gym bag and backpack, hailed an Uber, and snorted more coke in the back seat on the way to the vault. My driver eyed me dubiously but knew from the look of me not to say a goddamn word.

At the vault's front door, I scanned my palm, nodding to the security guard, then went to the iris scanner, which let me inside. I went and found Frank, who informed me of the situation. I was just standing there, drifting in and out of consciousness, my mind on the periphery of human perception. This was a movie. No, a video game. No, a slice of real life, an atom bomb dropped into a mud puddle, a vibration of sound and texture and light . . . why were the lights so fucking *bright*?

"You tell them anything?" I demanded.

Weaving, drifting, pacing, coming back.

"Of course not, dude," he said. "I don't even know your real name."

More questions, more words, all of it illusory and inconsequential. My life had boiled down to a precise yet foggy set of directives. His voice on my way out: "I'd be halfway to Mexico right now. . . ."

There was an idea.

From the vault, I grabbed all my cash, gold and silver bullion, valuables, and fake passports and IDs, stuffing them into my Louis Vuitton backpack and gym bag and dropping a few bars on the ground and hastily picking them back up. I had the one Phantom Secure phone with me, which I used to text El Jefe, saying I thought I would be coming to Mexico tomorrow morning. I didn't tell him why, although he probably already knew.

Another mad dash in ear-splitting traffic across the street to find that my Uber driver had bailed on me. With no phone to request a new driver, I ended up walking down Beverly Drive with 100 pounds of bullion, a quarter million in cash, and identities for three different countries. Within thirty minutes of practically dragging my bags back to Desiree's garage, I tossed the bags in the trunk of my Panemera and headed to Levi's house, my friend who had helped me launder money back in Australia. I took the elevator to his Marina Del Rey penthouse and Levi hefted my bag of ill-gotten gains like it was a fucking refrigerator, perspiration on his temples, his eyebrows creased under the strain. Was he nervous? Why was he nervous?

"Jesus," he said.

"I know."

"No, I mean *Jesus*, what the hell do you have in here, *barbells*?"

"Gold and silver." I glanced out his windows. *That black SUV, was it the same one I saw twenty minutes ago pulling out of the Wendy's parking lot right behind me?* "Give it to your brother and have him hold it for me. Have him put it in a safe or whatever, I don't care."

Before he could answer, I was back outside and climbed into the Porsche. Overhead, several helicopters. Were they tailing me? I'd never realized just how many helicopters were in the L.A. sky until today. And it seemed like they were all zeroing in solely on me. I had to get to the country club for tee-time at 7 a.m. That's right, I would meet with Al, play one last round of golf, then get the fuck out of there.

My mind was reeling, hands shaking, heart beating so fast I could hardly breathe.

Destroy the encrypted phone and go all the way to fucking Mexico. The cartel will take care of you. Yes, they're the same people who threatened to murder you a year ago, but they've seen your work; they know what you can do. You have earned their respect. All the same, it wasn't the most comfortable notion, that the only safe haven I had in the world was arguably under the roof of the world's most dangerous people.

At the country club, the entire parking lot was empty, aside from a truck with tinted windows. I didn't like the vibe, so I drove to the nearest McDonald's, where I got an Egg McMuffin and waited, my eyes studying every vehicle entering the lot.

I didn't want to admit it, but my daily intake of drugs and booze could paralyze a small elephant. It was nothing short of obscene. And the more I took, the more paranoid I became; the more paranoid I became, the more I took. Glancing around, I took a vial of coke from my jacket and had a bump. Just enough to settle my nerves. That's all this was, anyway. I was out of hand; I needed to check into rehab again. *That's what I'll do*, I decided in a flash of understanding. *I'll go meet Al, initiate the transfer, then head on over to Villa Oasis and check myself in.*

Content with this new plan, I drove back to the clubhouse and was relieved to see Al's car there. The golf caddy approached as I climbed from the Uber. "H-hello, Mr. Hanson. How are you, uh . . . doing today?"

I frowned. "Uh . . . good. How are *you* doing today? You good?"

The kid took my clubs from me.

"Fine, sir. Fine."

But I didn't like it. I stood there watching him walk away with my clubs, expecting me to follow, but I didn't. There was a rustling in the bushes, and I slowly turned my head. Two dozen uniformed agents sprang from the bushes with AR-15s drawn. "FREEZE! PUT YOUR HANDS BEHIND YOUR HEAD!"

Life suddenly went technicolor and slow-motion all at once. The agents ran toward me, but they moved slowly, as if trudging through mud. Even the drone of the police helicopters overhead was muted and distant and dulled like an underwater scream.

Whooosh . . . whooosh . . . whooosh.

All light was suddenly bright and blinding again, as if I'd been admitted to some perverse waiting room where the fluorescents were turned up to an ungodly opacity. I looked around as guns slowly rose into the air, their barrels pointed directly at me, the men holding them screaming words I didn't hear. I could see the muscles rippling in the arms of the agents running toward me; their cheeks jiggling, their dark sunglasses shielding their eyes from the sun that was now extraordinarily bright.

Closing my eyes, I raised my hands in the air and immediately felt them tugged behind my back and clamped in cold metal cuffs. Someone read me my rights. That's when I heard the accent—an Australian accent. It was then that I knew it was all over for me.

Al was rushed out of the clubhouse in handcuffs. He kept saying "Don't tell 'em a fucking thing, Owen! They got nothing on us!" But I knew he had done this. His arrest was all a ruse, and he had played the perfect part. I suddenly knew why he was all too eager to tip $800 on a $800 check—what did it matter, when Uncle Sam was footing the bill? I knew why he had plied Desiree with questions, and I understood that the vehicles in the Miami warehouse were just high-end drug-smuggling cars that had been confiscated by the feds. It all made sense. And in the midst of this, I realized I was going to prison for a very, very long time.

You might think I was afraid—afraid of prison, or of the cartel when they found out I'd been arrested. But that's the strangest thing; I wasn't afraid.

For the first time in so many years, I felt relieved.

EPILOGUE

The handcuffs were cold on my wrists.

Under the bright fluorescents of the typically spartan interrogation room, I felt like a creature trapped in an aquarium, but instead of lascivious little bastards peering in at me holding cotton candy and clutching their mom's skirts, it was the Feds.

Across from me was a long sheet of one-way glass, and I knew they were in there chatting amongst each other on just what to say, just what to ask . . . what perfect mode of speech and interview technique would fuck me, get me indicted on more charges than the litany of ones they already had against me. It was a game of chess, me sitting there with my cuffed hands on the cool metal table in front of me, trying not to feel the creeping intensity of my withdrawal from drugs and booze which had been a daily part of my regimen for years now. They knew this. And they had every intention of weaponizing it against me. Letting me sweat it out, giving me coffee instead of water just to ramp up the intense dehydration.

Make him slip. He will.

At first it was the Australians. They were friendlier, more diplomatic. They wanted to know how in the hell I had managed to get drugs into Fort Knox. It turned out they actually had done a great job of figuring out what all went down themselves. But I gave them nothing.

Then, it was the FBI. And they were a great deal more brass tacks than the Aussies. They drilled me with questions.

"Who was your boss from the cartel?" they asked.

I sat in the metal chair with the metal cuffs and the metal table, saying nothing. They tossed a file on the table, flicked it open. There were pictures of me in places I forgot I'd even been. Photographs of me meeting with some of El Jefe's men. They gave me some potential names of El Jefe. "Gentlemen," I said. "You know I'm not allowed to speak on these matters. You want to speak with anyone, then it's with my lawyer, James Henderson."

They showed me photographs of people who could be El Jefe. "Is this him?"

I remained silent.

"How about this guy, this him?"

"As I said. You will have to speak with my lawyer, James Henderson."

There was nothing they could say to compel me to rat out El Jefe. They knew I had a code of honor, and they also knew I would be a dead man if I ratted. They tried their last possible angle: witness protection.

Again, I said nothing.

"You're looking at decades behind bars, Mr. Hanson. Hell, once the Aussies get done with you and figure out their extradition proceedings, you probably won't see natural light until you're an old man. And do you think you've got protection behind bars? News flash buddy, you don't. You worked for the most powerful cartel in the world. What if the boss hears a little rumor that you're gonna turn? They can snuff you out in there any day of the week. How long is a white boy from Redondo Beach going to last in prison?"

I shrugged.

They left the room hastily.

Had the thought crossed my mind? Of course it had. And all those scenes from mob movies I saw as a kid came rearing their ugly heads. Maybe Henry Hill managed it for a while, until he was removed from the program for cocaine trafficking. But that was the Mafia. Right now, we were talking about the most dangerous drug cartel on earth. The FBI were kidding themselves. They didn't give a shit about my protection, they just wanted to take down El Jefe and look like the good ole boys.

Well, I wasn't going to help them do it.

RJ Cipriani.

The fucking guy with the ball cap and sunglasses and his Tumi suitcases, his square jaw and his paranoid head on a swivel, his Philly accent and arrogance. The guy who laundered money for the likes of me, lost it all, then hid behind his absurd moniker: Robin Hood. He was a good guy, a defender of the people and the downtrodden, an upstanding citizen and resolute voice in the arena of human morality. All of it a Fugazi. All of it stinking of bullshit.

Turns out, all those calls to the FBI had paid off, especially when they discovered I wasn't just laundering a couple million dollars of "fuck you" money. No. I was part of the most dangerous and powerful drug cartels on earth. The surfer boy from Redondo Beach, this USC athlete, this *güero* . . . he was the head of a massive international gambling operation that took bets from A-list celebrities, Super Bowl champs, World Series closers, and some of Mexico's most feared criminals. He was trafficking cocaine and narcotics by the ton across America, through Canada, and even into Australia, the Holy Grail of cocaine distribution. This California Kid sat at the head of an empire, and now he watched, slowly and ephemerally, while the walls came crashing inward as if from the omnipotent crushing force of a tsunami.

After I was sentenced to over twenty years and still faced an extradition to Australia, I was guided to a Bureau of Prisons bus, which took me to a United States Penitentiary in Lompoc, California. Los Angeles outside the wire mesh and glass seemed a world away from me, gleaming in the sun. Happy faces of children playing, of couples hand in hand on their way to date night, of old men and women ambling slowly and alone while carrying small bags of groceries. Of gangbangers and thugs drinking Modelo and tapping packs of cigarettes against their knees, sitting on car hoods with rap music blaring from improvised speakers. Faces of the forlorn and the forgotten, the many bedraggled rags of human beings curled up on sidewalks and under overpasses as the orange sun, glinting off the skyline, slanted and fell below the Pacific Ocean to the west and darkness crept over everything.

I wanted to cry.

I wanted to laugh.

To scream against the absurdity and the unreality of it all. None of it made sense, yet it made perfect sense. For some selfish reason I felt I was a victim of the system, and yet I was an oppressor. I had come so far in life, and yet I had utterly failed.

Was I ready for what came next?

Surely, I had to have played this scenario over in my head dozens, if not hundreds, of times. I knew the stakes of the game I was playing. Knew the risks and the rewards. Knew there were only a couple ways out: a cold tomb, or cold concrete walls. I'd won the latter, at the end of my game. Twenty-one years was my prize.

By the time I get out, my friends will have kids in college, retirement looming close. Many of the folks I knew will be gone. Will my dad still be alive? Will I ever get to see him on the outside again? If

I could get just one more round of golf with Big Jim. El Jefe . . . will he be dead, or the new acting boss of the cartel? Will I even make it to twenty-one years, or will I get stabbed during a prison riot?

No, I will not do anything deserving of that.

The cell was small, six by eight, and I shared it with Brock, a 6'6", four-hundred-pound white boy from Alabama. One of the first things he said to me was "In prison I only have my word and my balls, and I won't break them for nobody."

I nodded. "Neither will I."

My dad taught me honor. I had failed him; but in this way, I will never fail him. Like for him, my word is everything. I will honor the code of silence. Like in front of the house all those years ago when my mom and sister were driving away, as I was fighting back tears . . . I will not cry. I will take life as it is.

That's all I can possibly do.

ABOUT THE AUTHORS

OWEN HANSON has spent the past decade within the confines of the Federal Bureau of Prisons. Despite these challenges, he has achieved a significant academic milestone by earning his MBA from California Coast University during his incarceration. Prior to this, Hanson obtained his Bachelor of Science in Public Policy and Management from the University of Southern California (USC). At USC, he distinguished himself as a two-sport athlete, competing in both volleyball and football during the Pete Carroll era, a time highlighted by back-to-back national championships. Currently, Hanson is transitioning back into society, residing in a Federal Bureau of Prisons Halfway House in Los Angeles.

ALEX CODY FOSTER is the award-winning author of the true crime memoir, *The Man Who Hacked the World*, parts of which were included in the #1 Netflix film in the world at the time, *Running with the Devil: The Wild World of John McAfee*. He is the founder of Ghostwriting University.

```
LEGE FOOTBALL              124 GA TECH
AY OCTOBER 3               125 BWL GREEN
SS                         126 OHIO ST*      -34.5
          -6               127 KENT ST*      -24.5
                           128 TEMPLE*
DAY OCTOBER 4              129 BALL ST        -5.5
IDA                        130 BUFFALO
LL      -3.5               131 ARKANSAS
                           132 AUBURN          -16
Y OCTOBER 5               133 DUKE*
      -11                  134 ALABAMA*       -29
                           135 OKLA ST         -3
  -1                       136 KANSAS ST
                           137 TEXAS A&M    -1.5
                           138 KANSAS
CTOBER 6                  139 S DIEGO S
 -33                       140 BYU             -27
                           141 RICE            -2
                           142 TULANE
CTOBER 7                  143 NAVY
                           144 AIR FORCE -3
-20.5                      145 STANFORD
                           146 NTRE DAME -32
-11                        147 W VIRGINI -26
-6.5                       148 MISS ST
                           149 LSU             -2
7                          150 FLORIDA
8                          151 WASH ST         -4
                           152 OREGON ST
                           153 ARIZONA
```

```
.LEGE FOOTBALL          124 GA TECH
DAY OCTOBER 3           125 BWL GREEN
ISS                     126 OHIO ST*    -34.
        -6              127 KENT ST*    -24.
                        128 TEMPLE*
SDAY OCTOBER 4          129 BALL ST     -5.5
RIDA                    130 BUFFALO
LL     -3.5             131 ARKANSAS
                        132 AUBURN      -16
AY OCTOBER 5            133 DUKE*
        -11             134 ALABAMA*    -29
                        135 OKLA ST     -3
        -1              136 KANSAS ST
                        137 TEXAS A&M   -1.5
CTOBER 6                138 KANSAS
E -33                   139 S DIEGO S
*                       140 BYU         -27
                        141 RICE        -2
OCTOBER 7               142 TULANE
                        143 NAVY
        -20.5           144 AIR FORCE   -3
                        145 STANFORD
-11                     146 NTRE DAME   -32
-6.5                    147 W VIRGINI   -26
                        148 MISS ST
                        149 LSU         -2
7                       150 FLORIDA
16                      151 WASH ST     -4
                        152 OREGON ST
                        153 ARIZONA
```